THE SPIRIT OF ANI

THE SPIRIT OF ANI

REFLECTIONS ON SPIRITUALITY, FEMINISM, MUSIC & FREEDOM

BY **Ani DiFranco**
AND **Lauren Coyle Rosen**

BROOKLYN, NEW YORK
Publishing books since 1997

All rights reserved. No part of this book may be reproduced, stored in a retrieval system, or transmitted in any form, by any means, including mechanical, electronic, photocopying, recording, or otherwise, without the prior written consent of the publisher.

Published by Akashic Books
©2026 Ani DiFranco and Lauren Coyle Rosen

ISBN: 978-1-63614-277-7
Library of Congress Control Number: 2025941269
Second printing

EU Authorized Representative details:
Easy Access System Europe
Mustamäe tee 50, 10621 Tallinn, Estonia
gpsr.request@easproject.com

Akashic Books
Brooklyn, New York
Instagram, X, Facebook: AkashicBooks
www.akashicbooks.com
info@akashicbooks.com

Table of Contents

Introduction: Drop the Veils   9

Chapter 1:
    We Are All Apparitions   13

Chapter 2:
    The Illusion of Time and the Clairvoyance of Songs   29

Chapter 3:
    Gut-Brain vs. Head-Brain: How to Honor Our Intuition   45

Chapter 4:
    Telepathy, Feminism, and the Music Industry   59

Chapter 5:
    The Illusion of Self: How Ani DiFranco Doesn't Exist   73

Chapter 6:
    Spiritual Intentions and Manifesting Reality in Art and Life   89

Afterword: Visions for Our Times   105

Acknowledgments   107
Ani DiFranco's Discography   109
Books by Ani DiFranco   111
Book, Film, and Art References   112

Coda: Lyrics for Songs Referenced   115

Introduction

Drop the Veils

I think if I'm doing anything mentally before I go on,
it's: Drop the veils, drop the veils. Turn down the ego.
—Ani DiFranco

For Ani DiFranco, these veils are what separate her from others and from aspects of her full authentic self. They are like curtains that she seeks to part when she plays, so she can connect with her spirit through her music to all who wish to receive it. In many ways, this whole book is a beautiful dropping of the veils.

The driving pulse here is a look inside the spiritual, intuitive, and creative dimensions of Ani's work and presence, which have taken popular consciousness by storm since at least 1990, when she founded her own record label, Righteous Babe Records, and released her first album, the self-titled *Ani DiFranco*. As Ani shares in these chapters, she harbors and amplifies a consciousness of liberation as an ongoing and unending process rather than a destination. This is true for Ani's music, art, poetry, activism, feminism, and all other realms of her life.

How does this legendary folk-rock-and-much-else singer-songwriter and feminist icon summon her magic and work it to such versatile and transformative effect? What are her empowerment principles and practices, and how does her art relate to her spirituality? These are the questions *The Spirit of Ani* asks and answers.

I have been following Ani's music and poetry since I was fourteen in the late nineties, when my mother gave me a copy of the *Living in Clip* album. Not long after, I got the then-newest album, *Little Plastic Castle*. As I listened to them, worlds opened before me. I could sense realms and envision a creative life far beyond the confines of a pleasant yet subdued suburban Ohio. I felt energetically charged and spiritually activated in ways that I would only come to understand years later. I was vaguely aware that it was a variety of mystical experiences that I was having with her music. I did not so readily use those terms at that point in my life, but I *did* know that sonically imbibing her art took me to a space where I felt fortified, seen, and liberated as a young woman.

I knew I was one of countless others and that Ani had something deeply valuable and singular to offer us.

In early 2023, I reached out to Ani and her team to see if she might be interested in collaborating on a short book on her spirituality, art, intuition, and any mysticism that may be a part of her creative process and life. I am a cultural anthropologist and lawyer by training, and I am also a poet and artist. My research, teaching, and writing have focused on spirituality, art, consciousness, and liberation work for many years. In Ani's evocative and powerful best-selling memoir, *No Walls and the Recurring Dream*, I noticed multiple layers of spiritual and intuitive themes. For example, her conversation with the Goddess about the interplays of light and dark; or her reflections on waking from a trance to find a song written; or her explorations of the titular recurring dream of serving in the role of "ghost light" during concerts. A ghost light is one that lights a path for loving spirits and drives away negative energies that congregate in our public spaces. These moving and intriguing passages in Ani's memoir left me wishing to hear more from her about these aspects of her journey. To my great delight, Ani resonated with the idea of a book collaboration on the topic. Through a series of conversations in the winter and spring of 2023, we delved into these topics and then worked to sculpt this book in a spirit of genuine cocreation.

In the following chapters, Ani unlocks many of the mysteries of her creativity and philosophies. We cover terrain that sometimes remains enigmatic to Ani herself, at least in her conscious waking mind. She is open and vulnerable in these pages, as well as forthright and unapologetic. This is a signature Ani combination, which she has long used to great effect in her art. This powerful assemblage can be found across her breathtaking range of twenty-three studio albums, four live albums, and countless live bootlegs. It also runs through her profound published poetry and prose, and it animates her substantial and devoted following, which many have likened to a movement.

Ani's fierce independence and creative drive led to her pathbreaking work as one of the first people to found her own record label. Righteous Babe Records continues to flourish today, and all of Ani's albums have been released on it, despite mainstream record label efforts to bring her work into their catalogs. Her strong intuition guided her to stay the course of creative control and independence. This has further amplified her role as a guiding light to women, queer people, activists, and artists who wish to preserve the essence and integrity of their work in the face of unrelenting pressures to commodify, objectify, or otherwise submit to a foreign or alienating logic.

As with so many others who closely follow Ani and her work, she unveiled and mirrored for me parts of reality and of myself. She empowered me in formative years, and she helped me to find my own voice. Throughout the decades, Ani's art has remained a rejuvenating, alchemical touchstone, one whose meaning for me has transformed with my own spiritual evolution. I am thrilled to say that the process of expansion and liberation continued throughout the journey of writing this book with her.

So, let us begin with waking.

—*Lauren Coyle Rosen*

Chapter 1

We Are All Apparitions

The first time Ani and I spoke in voice, we met on Zoom. She opened the portal screen of her phone to what looked to me like the interior ceiling of a beautiful wooden-planked ship. She had arrived just a sliver past the hour. Something had awakened her, in the absence of an alarm.

"Two words: Advil PM," Ani said, laughing. "I feel like I left you at the Zoom altar."

I shared that my intuitive guidance had just told me to start by asking her what it feels like to be at the altar of song. Then, she signed on and spoke of a Zoom altar. This synchronicity duly sanctified the occasion for me. I took it as a sign from spirit that things were already on course.

"I should ask *you* what it's like being at the Zoom altar waiting on the little folk singer!" Ani replied.

She had been up late the night before, gardening in her backyard and grounding herself at her home in New Orleans, where she lives with her family. The full moon had hung overhead, amplifying her communion with her garden. This hum of energy is metonymic of Ani's broader existence as a conduit for electrifying words, songs, vibrations, frequencies, and spirit. Variations on the theme of Ani's transmission of energies would become a central theme over the course of our conversations about spirituality, life, philosophies, and creative journeys in music, poetry, painting, and other art forms.

The Spirit of Ani

I remarked that it was felicitous that Ani had just woken up. The way I see it, the veils are often thinner between the physical and spiritual worlds on either edge of sleep. There is something about the liminality of these zones that allows for clearer subconscious or spiritual communication.

"You're being very kind and generous," Ani said, laughing.

Ani and I then glided into our first conversation. I asked her about her sensorial experiences of music. I was wondering whether she, as with many other innovative and prolific musicians, has a broader suite of experiences with music than is commonplace—whether music, for her, has colors, tastes, textures, shapes, or scents. Does she see music either with her natural eyes or in her mind's eye? Does she feel music as she might experience touch or other tangible aspects of phenomena?

I also shared my experience of her music and performances as conveying spiritual electricity that is elevating, clearing, and activating. For me, this experience is true whether Ani is playing through studio recordings, through live audiovisual footage, or through live performances. I experience Ani's presence like a stream of energy that courses through the screen or through ambient projection via speakers. Her playing feels like a transmission of light that is alive and healing. Ani's playing also seems to transcend time, as the energy is activated afresh in the moment of listening to her music.

Ani speaks of the experience of songwriting as being in alignment and being a vessel for a transmission from beyond herself. I asked if a kindred experience of opening, aligning, and receiving sometimes happens when she plays onstage. I also wondered whether all of this has changed over the years, with her own morphing perspectives or shifts of consciousness.

I very much feel the spirit moving through you when you're onstage. At least, it feels that way to me.

Well, I'll just tell you the first thing that comes to mind. I feel amazed that that is true because you feel it, and other people feel it. For me, my mind is really busy much of the time worrying, doubting myself, beating myself up, thinking that I look like shit, that I didn't say that thing right, that I'm not singing well or whatever. Then, it's the same thing when I look at my recordings. I think, *Oh God, that sucks, and that sucks. That's cringey, and that's insanely cringey.*

I feel deep, burning regret and shame. And yet, in all these moments, in all these songs—recorded or live—people are connecting. People are present there with me. I have to just trust that somehow, even though I know I suck [*laughs*], that there's something coming through me that's real or useful, because other people are connecting with it. I have to believe that's what counts. Not whether you suck or not, but that somehow there's a meaning, something to what I'm doing—that makes sense. Because other people find healing in it, find joy in it, find themselves in it. It blows my mind that that's the case. Sometimes I look or listen to myself, and I think, *Oh . . . no* [*laughs*]. But then, other people look or listen to me, and they think, *Yes. Thank you.* That makes it all okay.

Maybe it's the recognition that others experience. There's a synergy, or something like a mirroring, which helps people experience something in themselves.

Yeah, for me, on some level, it might be, *Oh, the affirmation that I crave. Okay, yay, mission accomplished.* But I'm even talking about something beyond a kind of ego-boosting affirmation. More like a recognition of interconnectedness, through the songs, or through the energy field that I create when I play or when I step onstage. I have to trust that it is a process that's taking place through both of us that just *is*, that can't be judged. I judge myself a lot. I often don't feel good about myself or about what I'm doing in any given moment, but the fact that it's connecting, the fact that somehow other people seem to feel that I'm really there with and for them—I have to take faith in that. And I do. It's a great joy to me that this work that I do can help other people, can inspire other people, can uplift them—even though somehow, I don't manage to do that for myself.

Is there a way to describe your states of consciousness onstage, if you fade in and out? I know people often don't necessarily talk about it, but many artists will have different levels of consciousness or awareness while playing onstage or writing. Is there a way of talking about these altered states that you feel comfortable with? I know you specifically talked about songwriting in your recent memoir. You mentioned that you'll go out, you'll go into a trance, and then you'll wake up, and you'll feel so grateful that you've taken some pain or something that was maybe heavy, and you've transformed it, made it into something else. You gave the pain a rebirth, or you birthed it and sent it out into the world as a song. I was wondering at what point, if you recall, was that part of your journey unlocked for you on a conscious level?

Yeah, I think that's all that making music is for me. It's the ignition of that subconscious or extra-conscious level. I think my conscious mind is pretty locked up a lot of the time with self-loathing and worry. But I think right from the beginning of finding the guitar at nine, the guitar became a spaceship that I could take somewhere far, far away from that—far away from my nine-year-old troubles, or my fifty-two-year-old troubles. It still runs! That spaceship still goes [*laughs*].

Yesterday, there was a lady on the corner of my block who spent several hours sort of dancing, sort of flailing up and down the block, screaming, cursing angrily, obviously very agitated. I don't know if there were some substances involved or if she was just in a manic episode or what was happening with this lady. She was screaming, and my friend who lives next door, we were talking later, and she said, "I woke up to the screaming, and it was like some sort of apparition."

And I thought, *That's exactly what it is. It's the apparition of pain and suffering and agitation and stress.* In that sense, we're all apparitions, in any given moment. Things move through us, all of us, all the time. It's the generosity of the world. It's the unconditional love of the world. Or it's the violence of the world, the pain—all of these energies that we embody, that embody us. That move through us.

I think about how much we as humans live in the ego. We're so convinced of our selfhood and our identity. We think we're these individuals, creating things. I'm not a meditator yet, per se, but I've had the experience, in creating art, where you actually put down the ego and just become a conduit for something. It's so freeing. I think I have heard meditators and gurus talk about how freeing it is to lose the illusion of being a person with an identity that has to do stuff. I think, going back to what I was saying about being caught up in my inadequacy, it's so freeing to just push through that and realize that I don't have to be good at anything. I don't have to look good or sound good. I just have to be open and present. Open and available for the goodness of the world to possibly move through me.

In your new song "The Knowing" [accompanying Ani's first children's book by the same name, published in early 2023], you sing, "underneath all that i know is the knowing." For me, that speaks to this interconnectedness beyond the illusions of separateness. It speaks to the connectedness of everything, of consciousness, and how consciousness is like a pathway or a network.

Yeah, sometimes I don't feel like I believe or have faith in my ability to put my antenna up and receive things and share them. Or I don't know if I'm doing it effectively. So, I just have to trust that somehow, even with my inadequacies, something good happens. Things are coming through, and things are finding their way to whoever needs them. Sometimes I wish that I could do things better and sound better, and that things would be more effective. But then, I just have to trust that what's coming through is coming through, and the people it's reaching are the people it's meant to reach, and I should just relax about the process.

When you are speaking your truth and your authenticity, your power just lights up. It activates an energy field for me, and I'm sure for many others, too. Do you get that activation or sense, like tingling vibrations, when you're listening to certain music or listening to particular people speak?

Definitely. I absolutely know what you're talking about. Listening to music, for sure, when people really open themselves and show themselves through the sound. Also, just being around people that are tapped-in in some way that I relish or crave. There are people who I just want to be around because there's something about their energy field that is a solace or an inspiration.

I love how you identify that ineffable quality with the divine feminine in your memoir, in the chapter "The Alphabet v. the Goddess" [inspired by the 1998 book The Alphabet Versus the Goddess *by Leonard Shlain]. I really like how you were saying that the feminine principle is about not having to be so individuated and discrete, so articulable and abstract. Language is everywhere and can be close to things, but it is already an abstraction.*

Precisely.

Often when I write, I don't think about it much in advance. Or that's the best-case scenario, I guess. Is it like that with music for you? I know you said that sometimes you'll go into a trance, and you'll receive music, but if you're fully awake, is it sometimes almost like something is playing your fingers?

Yes, totally. I don't have control in the way that—well, on some level, you practice guitar, and you play and play and play for years and years, and you develop fine motor control and the ability to play. But on another level, it's really not that way. I'm completely not in control. I've learned how to play so I can go at it onstage and start playing guitar or start singing. But really, I have the sensation of being a bystander and at the mercy of something bigger. I think I talked about it in my memoir, of not being in control at all. On some other level, I'm sort of just standing there listening to it, like anybody else.

Sometimes, I listen to my guitar, and I'm like, *Yeah, let's go. Alright. Whoa.* It's just in this really open, free, unfettered zone. Other times, my hands are just struggling, and I can't fix it. Same thing with the voice. I open my mouth, and sometimes what comes out is coming from my soul or from whatever. It's just coming through, and it's free, and it's open, and it's absolute—visible and audible—there's this open channel that things can be seen and heard through.

Other times, it's just notes and words, it's cloudy. I imagine that, in those moments, you can hear the self-doubt, you can hear the fear and the worry. You can hear layers and veils of ego. No matter how much I practice making music or giving music, I can't learn how to just mechanically lift the veils when they fall across my voice or between me and the person I'm singing to. It just is. So yeah, I often don't feel like I'm in control on that level.

So, it's not as though you can just summon the openness, and then you go to the side and bear witness to the process or something like that? It just comes unbeckoned?

Well, it does feel like, if I stay onstage long enough and point myself toward it, the veils will probably fall eventually. I guess in that sense, it is very much a practice. You just keep sitting there, and you keep acknowledging the thoughts, and you keep doing it, and maybe eventually, there will be clarity. Some nights, I can walk out onstage and *boom*, I'm just there, I'm present, I'm available. Or whatever it is that I'm working with is available to me. Other nights, it's a long journey to try to get to that place. I've learned to be patient and just let it unfold. It always sucks to do a three-song set or something, if you're doing a benefit or a multi-artist bill, and you get three songs to get there, to be open and clear [*laughs*]. That's tough because it often takes me longer.

When you come back in, is it to your full everydayness? Is it kind of just like breathing—you breathe back, and then you're there, and then maybe your body is tired?

I wish it was like that! *Okay, now exhale, and now move on to the next thing.* That sounds very healthy [*laughs*]. It's not like that. I've had to really work at incorporating the experience more quickly and recovering, because I find that being onstage is sort of an extreme level of giving out and taking in energy. But I'm the kind of person who experiences just going to the grocery store as very stimulating emotionally. Just interacting with people leaves me with a lot that

I have a really hard time putting down. After every performance, I just have so much to process. They're just different flavors of interaction, the relationship with the audience when I'm onstage, or one-on-one, or in a smaller group. But each of them leaves me so stimulated with other people's energies, with probably what I picked up of the world around me—of pain or need or hunger or thirst—even just the positive things leave me reeling. When I get offstage, usually what I like to do is keep playing, to sort of try to move through it.

This reminds me of shamanism, or the work of priestesses and priests who are mediums, how they somatize some of other people's energies for them in order to heal them or to lift and transmute the energies for them. As they do so, they often take on many of the feelings of the energies, or the symptoms or sensations that others are having, in order to then shift the feelings and energies out. I wonder if, for you, that's just part of your avatar, part of the service you provide to humanity, and part of why everyone feels so uplifted and opened and enlightened and elevated when they leave a show. Maybe it's partly because you've just taken all of that for them. But then, you come back into your full consciousness, and it's like, Oh, I have to shed all this stuff. Stuff that might be coming from a whole theater auditorium. *That must be really intense.*

Super intense. And I don't really understand it. It's a thing that happens that I don't understand. And I get the sense that it's a process that has probably always happened for me, on some level. When I was a kid, I was very tuned in to other people, feeling them—and really not wanting them to hurt. Maybe I also developed people-pleasing skills and survival skills as an emancipated minor that involved making other people feel good, but I think it goes deeper than that. I can feel it's not just self-serving—or a calculation for my benefit. I guess when you're feeling other people's pain with them, it's *your* pain. You want to make it better.

A lot of people go into a period of life where they're more encased, or where they're not consciously picking up as much from others—perhaps in their teens or twenties. It seems like you maybe didn't have that period. Maybe it is because you went right into the authenticity of your soul-space with the art at such a young age. You mentioned the first benefit concert you played as a kid, the one with Michael, your guitar teacher and friend.

Yeah, I started playing for people publicly when I was nine—right away. I think that benefit concert that I talked about in the memoir, to save the whales and dolphins, was on my eleventh birthday. I had already been performing regularly.

That must have been so intense. You had no walls in your house with your parents and brother, growing up. I feel like that's symbolic of the broader situation. You were just thrown, feet to the fire, into the world of human adulthood, with all the beauty but all the completely crazy stuff, too.

Yes, taking in everything from the people around me. Also, the nakedness of my role in that process is really hard to adapt to. Another thing that leaves me reeling after every experience is feeling like not only is everybody's stuff coming in, but *my* stuff is also pouring out onto the whole freaking world. You're an open book. I feel the vulnerability hangover intensely. When I get offstage—to go back to that moment—that's another thing that I'm reeling from, being so exposed.

How do you center and ground afterward?

I was in my garden till midnight last night, moving a garden bed from one place to another. It was the full moon, and it was a beautiful night. I had had people over for dinner, dear friends, so that was awesome, but I was so buzzed from the conversation. And then at midnight, I'm like, *I'm supposed to wake up at six thirty.* And I knew I wasn't going to be able to sleep, so that's where the Advil PM came in. But I was so happy. I think I'm the most at peace in my garden when I'm working in the dirt. It's very literally grounding for me. And water, for sure. There's something so deeply soothing about being by water. I love living in Louisiana, where the air is so full of water. We have the Mississippi about four blocks away here [in

New Orleans]. It's a little hard to get close to it because of all the stuff in the way, at this part of the river. But yeah, I like to ride my bike up and down the bike trail that goes along the levee.

Do you hear music in the river or in the garden or, say, in people's eyes?

No, not per se. Sometimes I have thoughts when I'm out and about or interacting or doing something else that lead to songs, but I don't exactly hear music in these other activities. It will lead to music, but it's more like the energetic seed of a song. People always ask, "Is it words first or music first?" Of course, it's different all the time, but I think that what's really first is a feeling, a frequency. When you tap into something that you want to express, on an energetic level, then you find the words and the sounds to go with it. I think, for me, songs usually start with a feeling.

So it's a frequency or a vibration that you might feel from the river, say, and then you can convert that into a song?

Yeah.

Do you get that from, say, paintings or people, basically from everything?

Certainly, when I was younger, I would get it from everything all the time, everywhere. The songs come fewer and further between now, maybe just because I have so many other things going on. I have kids, and I have so many other responsibilities and things that take my mental space and my time and my energy. But yeah, I think when I was younger, it was just constantly showing up.

Do you remember a moment when you had a spiritual awakening, or something you would call a spiritual awakening? Or was it always just that you were open with these expansive perceptual faculties?

I don't recall any moment. For me, it's more like a state of being or a story that unfolds. It's not one moment.

Do you have patterns or experiences of what people call dark nights of the soul? Do you have experiences where you come out of something and feel like you're reborn into something else?

Yeah. Grief, for instance, is very regenerative, the way fire is regenerative. It burns down whatever you were. Then, you rise from what's left. I have a respect and even affection for my grief, because when I'm really hurting like that, there are no veils. There is nothing to work through. There's nothing to overcome, no journey to get there. You're just completely cracked open in a way that can't be clouded. Nor can it be safe and secure! But there's almost a calm in it, because it's completely out of your hands.

I had this moment when I was touring last week. I can't remember where I was, but I was onstage and I was talking about a song I was going to play, from the record *Educated Guess* [released in 2004], which I made deep, deep in the backswing of my Saturn return. I was having a period of years where I was really struggling. I had just blown up my first marriage, and I was confronting a lot of things that I had been avoiding about my life and my trauma coming up. My dad died, and he was the vessel of unconditional love that I'd always known. Anyway, I was going to play this song from *Educated Guess*, which was this record I made alone at home while slitting my wrists, you know [*laughs*]. I didn't say all of that, but I said something about this album that I made while coming undone, and somebody in the back of the theater said, almost in a quiet way and yet I heard it, "Thank you for that." I made that record while grieving the loss of my father, grieving the loss of my marriage, and somebody took the opportunity to make a sound in my direction that squeezed my hand and met my eye. I started playing the song, and I was crying quietly to myself, just for the acknowledgment and the feeling of connection. This person, this one spry individual, who took the opportunity to say, "Thanks for being available to me, pal, even in your grief. Thanks for reaching out and sharing it and showing it. That helped me."

That's what I heard, anyway. There are so many little moments onstage of every flavor that hit so deep with me. They come in all kinds. Some are beautiful, and some are brutal. But I've got to say: my audience, the people that come out to hear me—there's so much love and support and deep listening. I'm lucky that a lot of the affecting moments fall in those realms.

I listened the other night to this song and interview you did for Google a few years back, where your daughter, Petah, joined you in singing. In the Q&A, this guy said that he was one of the people who would not be here without your music. Your music got him through his teenage years in Idaho, I think it was. I started crying in the kitchen. I was cooking as I was listening to this Q&A. I thought, to hear that once would mean the world to me. Music like yours is medicine.

Yeah, I've been blessed for many years now to hear that feedback, that response of, "You got me through," or, "You got me all the way to myself." And that's exactly what it means to me: the world. It still does. It never gets old. That is it. I feel like that is why I'm here. Or, at least, why I'm an artist. That shows me the purpose of my art. I feel very sound about that. There's nothing, there's no greater reward for me than to just—for all the work I put in and the stuff that I do, all the struggle that's involved—to look in somebody else's eyes and for them to say, "I'm alive because of you." Then I'm like, *Okay, next gig! Next one! Pick up that hammer, that next nail, thumbs be damned!*

One thing that really struck me when traveling through your memoir was your ability to summon senses of power and protection wherever you may be, including sleeping alone outside. Especially as a woman, I have to say it was amazing to read that you slept alone in a bus or train station on what you called your sweet sixteen, your sixteenth birthday. You said something about summoning your stand-back vibe, like a force field around you.

Yeah, I refuse to live in fear of any kind. I'm not really into locks. Maybe it's a physical manifestation of being available to the world.

Maybe the disinclination for locks is a representation of your desire to always remain unlocked with everything, including your music and other art. When you paint, is that also in an altered state?

It can be. I've been so far from painting for many years, but I remember, back when I was doing it a lot, being able to enter that state where you can look at a blank page or canvas, but you can see things, and then you just have to copy them over. The things you're seeing. That's that state.

So, you'll see an outline or something?

Yeah, where you can picture a thing. That's when it's really working, I think. I have experienced that analogous state in visual art in the past, but it has been a long time.

When you receive your songs and you're awake, do you get a visual feed in your mind's eye? Or it just comes into your ears, or it comes to your fingers? Or it just totally varies?

I think the sense of the song comes more to my spirit, to my soul. It's like an intuitive understanding of some energy. And then I experiment with words, and I experiment with chords and sounds, and when something feels right, then I start going with that. But it comes from the feeling first. Then, if the sound is matching it, I'll hear it. There was a little more randomness in the process earlier on, but also, I think, more openness in me, so it would connect up and work more often than not, or enough of the time. But there were also some times when I would just go with a sound or some words because I became attached to them, even though maybe they weren't quite right. I feel like I've gotten more in touch with, *Yes, this actually fits.* Not bringing the wrong melody or the wrong music to the intention behind a song.

In your memoir, when you were talking about Prince, you spoke of how, in your experience, you felt that his spirit was so large or vibrant that it would seem to leak through his body. It was such a vivid description. Do you ever feel that way about your spirit? Do you ever feel your spirit, say, enter plants or the air? Can you regularly feel your spirit exceeding your body?

I do feel like I connect with other beings that are not necessarily humans. I want to evolve to do that more and more, if I can guide myself there. When I was a kid, my best friend, my most solid companion, was a cat. We had two cats, and one of them, we had a really deep connection. It's funny, I didn't write about her at all in my book. But the older I get, the more I sort of try to open myself to connections. I love sitting out on the porch with my guitar and playing and being aware of what birds come and hang out, and maybe hanging out and singing with them, not singing *over* them. Wondering about how they hear my music, and how much they, too, are intending to sing with me, or what. Or listening to crickets stop singing when you come near, and then trying to regain their trust enough to get an up-close, front-row seat to their show. All of those things.

When I started planting things and working with trees and other plants, I started tapping into their nature, as species and as individuals, their ways of being. A plant in a pot is an easy thing to move around, but it's isolated and at the mercy of its human captor. I love plants. I love trees. I love watching things grow and mature. I love assisting and nurturing and also just watching, over time. Some trees are super wild, and they're all over the place, and some are so symmetrical and controlled and purposeful. Just seeing those different energies manifest and adapt and face adversities is fascinating. But a plant in a pot, it's like, *Wow. When I had it over there, it was struggling. It was suffering. Over here, look at how much happier it is*. I like feeling that stuff, just tuning in to the needs of a plant and what it's expressing. I really dig it. I think of it in terms of paying attention, but I hope that there's something in my spirit that is palpable, that is felt as responsive to them.

Absolutely, the spirits and languages of plants are such complex and beautiful forces to behold.

I feel that even rocks are alive, conscious, in a very *proto* way. I feel they are the oldest form of consciousness around. It's so remote from the kind that you and I embody that it's extremely easy to dismiss. I think most humans, at least in this society, dismiss the consciousness of plants, let alone stones. We dismiss the consciousness of other humans! But I feel like stones are the first proto-creation of embodied consciousness, and then it kept evolving. Consciousness became more sophisticated, more active, even more "alive."

I have rocks that I've carried with me from many of the places I've lived. And they're heavy! I was just moving them last night, in my garden under the full moon. When I left my house in Buffalo, I just couldn't leave these big stones behind. They were my fellow travelers already, and I've moved them like three or four times now! I laugh to think of the blip of their time with me. Sitting there for thousands of years, and then, *boom*! "We're moving to New Orleans!" Seriously. I don't even know how many pounds of rocks I've moved. They're like the size of dishes. Or toaster ovens. They're various sizes, but they're totally part of my stuff.

Do you ever sit on them or, no, that would not be respectful?

No, I don't sit on them, but they're pet rocks, and I put them next to my plants. I literally have rock friends that are more my speed. When I hang out with my rock friends, I don't feel overwhelmed [*laughs*].

Do they emit a certain frequency, or do they lift things off of you? If you want to ground and get rid of whatever energy you picked up from the grocery store, do you ever sit with the rocks?

Up in Canada, where I go in the summer, or whenever I can, where my mother lives, there are a lot of rocks, and they're big. Sometimes you can just see this one part of them, but they go very deep down. It's always amazing to me that in the middle of the summer, when it's a really hot day, you can put your hand on some rocks and they're cold. Because they're going so deep into the earth. I love to go and lay my hands on certain rocks and mosses. I'm huge into mosses and lichen and mushrooms and all the ancient ones. To me, it's all magical and mysterious—these beings that contain intelligences that are so different—really trying to open up my intuitive knowing enough to hear them, see them, understand.

When you put your hands on the rocks, do you receive energy through your hands?

Yeah, I feel like I do. And like I'm able to sense, by touching the surface, way deep into the earth. The rocks are going way deep down in there and bringing up messages, bringing up wisdom.

Chapter 2

The Illusion of Time and the Clairvoyance of Songs

Our second conversation opened with the matter of dreams. I asked Ani whether she recalled her dreams, thinking that she may draw spiritual and musical inspiration from them. She and I had conversed at length the evening before, in my dream state. When I woke up, I felt sure that the dream space had been full of wise guidance for our waking conversation. If only I could have remembered the contents! Ani did not remember any such dream and could not retrieve the information either, alas.

Ani's beloved dog Lefty joined us at her side for the duration. We traversed myriad topics—from entering timeless spaces through the portal of music, to tapping into spirit for creating songs and poems, to Ani's clairvoyance in the valences and messages of her works, whose meanings and prophecies often don't disclose themselves until years later. Ani shared how she prefers to write alone, because it allows her to zero in on the gossamer threads and elusive subtle energies that help to give birth to her songs. When she's among others, jamming or otherwise, it is hard to maintain the inward focus that this type of deep connection requires.

We spoke about Ani's childhood experiences with feeling imperiled or unsettled, which she understands to have given rise to many of her intuitive capacities to read other people—to sense the thoughts, feelings, and intentions beneath the surface level of what someone is saying, doing, or presenting. As a highly intuitive child, she often picked up others' energies without understanding why, and it would feel overwhelming and sometimes enervating.

Since Ani got her first guitar at age nine, the instrument has been a vessel that allows her to transcend uncomfortable circumstances. Music is an elevating and clarifying escape from the morass. By playing, Ani can work through the discordant energies she has accumulated. This revitalizes, recharges, and heals her, which in turn allows her to create the healing and transformative music she shares with the world.

Do you remember your dreams a lot?

No, not really. I wish I did.

I was just wondering because you came through in a dream to me last night, very extensively [laughs]. I don't remember it all, but we were conversing at length. Also, you played somewhere, I think it might have been my high school. It was a place where you wouldn't have played. It felt like more of a convergence of the energies for the collaboration, which is great. I woke up feeling more connected.

That's funny. I'm curious what I said in your dream. If only we could have the transcript [*laughs*].

Yeah, I could ask spirit to send it through [laughs]. I think the cool thing is the sense that we're pulling through or manifesting something that already exists in the spiritual realm, bringing it into the physical realm. You seem very nonjudgmental.

I try to be. I think that, if you live long enough, you've got to be. I feel that way. You realize that thinking critically about other people is just a mistake, because then it's time for you to suck and turn all that criticism on yourself . . . Yeah. It's like that. Compassion is just a better habit to have. I feel like I spent a lot of years in that ping-pong: *You suck. No, I suck!* Until, I was like, *Enough! Nobody sucks. Nobody.*

It's so great that Lefty came to join us. Is there a meaning to share behind her name?

Oh, well, we have this other dog named Pancho. You know that Townes Van Zandt song that Willie Nelson made famous, "Pancho and Lefty"? When she came along, we decided to go with that.

Last time, you spoke a bit about the cat you had as a kid. I was wondering if you could say more about your relationship with your cat when you were little, if you feel comfortable.

Yeah, I named her Frisky. We had this cat that had kittens and then we kept one of them, Frisky. But unfortunately, it was not amicable between the mother cat and the daughter cat [*laughs*]. The mother cat did not appreciate her daughter staying in her territory, I guess, and being a permanent part of the household as well. She was always attacking Frisky.

Who knows, maybe Frisky and I related to each other because of feeling not comfortable in our home or something [*laughs*]. But yeah, Frisky would sleep in the bed with me, but not curled up next to me—we slept hugging. She'd put one arm around either side of my neck and rest her neck across mine. I'd be lying on one side, and when I would flip over, she would flip over with me. I'd roll her over my chest, and we'd switch sides. That's how we slept. I just relate to cats in general. They're very independent, very thoughtful. It's funny how cats have so much embarrassment and shame. Did you ever see an embarrassed cat? They get embarrassed easily.

It's very palpable [*laughs*]. If a cat slips or falls or does something awkward, they get embarrassed, which seems like a very sophisticated social emotion. Many people don't assign any emotions at all to animals, which is kind of insane. But cats, anyway, they have this whole capacity for shame that I relate to. And just basically existential thinking.

Could you talk to Frisky easily? Would you just get her, what she was communicating?

I remember us being really tight. Cats are not like dogs, they don't follow you around necessarily, but this cat and I, we hung out a lot. The sad postscript to that story is that when I left that house, my parents' house, when I was eleven, I went to live with my mom in an apartment where we couldn't have pets. And shortly after I moved out, Frisky just disappeared. My dad and brother still lived in the house, so she could've stayed, but she didn't. I never knew what happened to her. I always felt really sad about abandoning her. It's a hole in my heart, which is probably why I didn't even write about her in my book. Even now, it's like, my little cat friend—my first real friend—life took me away from her. I never saw her again or knew what happened to her.

Are there certain moments, such as these—having Frisky, losing Frisky—that you recall from childhood that are still an active part of you that you tap into as a wellspring for your creations?

Sure, tapping into emotional signposts from the past. I think I pretty much carry it all with me. Like any person, I'm still trying to untangle myself from the early stuff. I think I have been processing it for a lot of years, in the book and in all those songs, especially in the songs. A song is not a thing you just do once and sing once. You sing it again and again and again and again. In a way, you're forced to revisit and revisit moments and feelings. It's an interesting sort of practice to write songs and then sing them repeatedly, over and over for years. Some of them, anyway—some more than others.

But does this help move through things? I hope—sort of, sometimes. It definitely means you can't leave it in the realm of denial or not addressing it. To write about it and to sing it over and over again means you are really looking at it. Like the judgment thing we were talking about earlier—repeatedly singing something can lead me to a place where I'm eventually like, *Enough!* And then there's a shift within me. It forces me to shift my relationship to things.

Is it painful when you play a song that has been written from a place of trauma or pain? Or, at that point, has it already been transmuted into a kind of medicinal thing for you that you're then also sharing with people?

It can be painful, especially when it's fresh, definitely. Sometimes, I can't play songs in a show because it will be too triggering for me, and crying onstage sucks. I've done it plenty. And then sometimes, the pain in a song or the drama in a song is just not something I feel anymore, so it doesn't feel natural to sing from that place. Usually, the process puts a little bit of distance, as it goes along, between the initial inspiration of a song and you. You put distance between yourself and the event or feeling that inspired it, and then you just have a relationship with the song itself—with the interpretation of the pain—the art that came from it. I guess that's like in any memory—it's just a musical version. You really forget the initial thing, you just remember the remembering. But the song itself has a life, so you're in relationship with that more than anything.

Is there a reason why you chose to have a tree on the cover of your new children's book, The Knowing?

Well, I didn't choose it, actually. That was the choice of the artist. But I really like that cover. It's beautiful. I was hoping to do the artwork for the book myself, but the publisher who offered me the deal wanted to pull in a different artist, so they found Julia [Mathew]. It was cool to see my story interpreted through somebody else. Julia's paintings are really beautiful. She brought a whole other cultural element. They asked me if I wanted to give her direction, and I basically said, "No, I want her to bring herself. Here are the words. Here's what I'm saying. You interpret it through your lens." She made the pictures without me telling her what to draw.

So, people tap into that—the knowing of the essence of things—and then what they generate tends to come out in a way that echoes or somehow represents the truth of whatever you're transmitting from your spirit, right?

Yeah, sure. I just wanted her to be led and informed by her own knowing. I think a lot of times in art—with music, I've had the experience where I have an idea in my head of what the bass sounds like, or how this or that should sound, and I try to get another musician to do that idea. I mean, it can work, but it can also end up that nobody's spirit is really coming through. Another person can't necessarily play my idea in a way that sounds all the way authentic to them. So, I usually find it's better for them to come with their own idea. Generally, in life, I prefer to hear what comes out of other people instead of telling them what to play. I'm like a jazz musician in that way. In some ways, the song is merely the subject of a conversation.

Even in your bands, with the people who play in them?

Yeah. I mostly show them how a song goes, and they interpret it. I might say, "Ooh, I like this better than that," or, "Ooh, I love that." But it's not about dictating to other people how to interpret it. It's just about being in the dialogue with one another. The important part of that equation is getting in the room with people who have something of their own to say, and then just trusting them. You have to make sure you have the right people involved, so you can do that. So you're free to have a real conversation.

Do you sometimes just jam with a band and experiment on a song, and even start with only, say, a chord progression or something, and say, "Just play what feels right"—kind of like Miles Davis and all the great masters of improvisational flows?

Well, I don't usually write songs by jamming with other people so much. I mean, I've tried it along the way, but for me it's not the most effective path. I guess I might bring something that's in process out, in sound check, to see what it feels like with the band. But usually, if I'm bringing it to the band, it's pretty well formed. Maybe not all the way finished, but for me, writing songs takes so much focus, and it's really about getting super in-touch with something. The act of playing with other people and interacting with them and jamming, that's a few steps removed from that kind of focus. For me, it's about really honing in on something that's very tenuous and very delicate. If you move your head at all, you might lose it, this thing that's very elusive and hard to focus on in a sustained way. It's about trying to get closer to it, like a wild animal, without chasing it away. I think it's just the way that I write, the intuitive level that I'm trying to tap into with the lyrics and whatever.

There are so many different ways of writing. It's funny to me that some pop performers are considered songwriters—and, I mean, they *are* songwriters in a different mode—but the songs are cowrites. They get in the room with pros, with people who know how to round off rough edges and tie it up with a bow and do all the things. And what comes out is very effective but somewhat different in nature from what I do. It feels like it's one step away from "art for art's sake" and toward a product.

Yeah, people like Jack Antonoff, who frequently cowrite with other pop artists, helping to fashion and produce things.

I don't mean to diss it. Like all art needs to be the same thing or come about in the same way. Where would the world be without those anthemic pop songs? Those songs and those processes are cool, but I guess I'm biased toward the unhomogenized milk, straight out the teat! [*Laughs*] I guess I just experience that collaborative song-crafting space as a whole other thing. I've done a little bit of it—cowriting, trying to craft a song with someone. But for me, the mode that I am usually in, with writing, necessitates a lot of space and quiet.

The way you describe it, along with the serene vibe in your voice and energy right now, all of this reminds me of the deep, inward feeling of your song "Everest" [from the 1999 album Up Up Up Up Up Up]. *For me, that song is perfect. It always brings me to that place of the totality of everything, but not the collapsing or vacuum-like void aspect of the totality. It's the peaceful, harmonious homeostasis of totality. It brings me to a very inward, contemplative space as I listen. Is "Everest" an example of a song that originally came through while you were in a trance, in an altered state, while you were a vessel for spirit?*

I think so. I think it came through that way. With a song like "Everest," if I was in a room with other people trying to jam on things or come up with stuff together, those other people are not going to know what *that*—the kernel of truth or experience—what that *exact* everything is about. That feeling that you just described, that's exactly what I was trying to express, so it makes me happy to hear you say that. The song came out of a memory of being in this faraway place, in a very different culture, and making a friend across a big cultural divide, and having them take me to church with them. So I would be the only one in the [songwriting] room with that particular experience that I was using to bring this feeling forward. I can't imagine trying to write "Everest" by spitballing with other people.

I've never climbed Mount Everest. I've never been to the top of it, but I feel as though I've been there in spirit. The song also gives me a sense of the intuitive sensations of everything flowing in smoothness and in harmony, despite differences that may appear jagged or even insurmountable, from certain vantage points. You sing:

> from the depth of the pacific
> to the height of everest
> and still the world is smoother
> than a shiny ball bearing
> so, i take a few steps back
> put on a wider lens
> and it changes your skin
> your sex and what you're wearing . . .

It's so beautiful. Actually, have you been to Mount Everest?

No, I haven't. The title just comes from the idea that these distances that seem so huge—like, from the Mariana Trench to the height of Everest—if you step back just a little bit, get in your spaceship and look down, those differences are actually minute. It's about relating to everything, to other people, like we're actually one thing. And if you just step back, maybe the differences that seem so vast and insurmountable are not so.

"Everest" carries the feeling of this cosmic wisdom that there's no need to go anywhere or have anything in particular, if you already are that or you already are there. As one with all.

Yeah, "Everest" came from that feeling of just *being* and of feeling connected. Like, it's all pretty damn great as it is.

You were telling me how your guitar, ever since you started playing it, would bring you to this place where everything is okay. It would take you out of your mind chatter that was running, either in the foreground or in the background of your thoughts and feelings. And it would lift you out of any heavy energy you were picking up from people around you, including your family. Is it possible to share a bit about what the guitar-as-spaceship was like for you? Did it vertically launch you out of all of that?

Right. The ultimate escape that could just take you really far away. I think I was pretty invested in the idea of escape when I was a kid, because I think I felt pretty trapped in things that were not of my design. When people are in relationships that are not healthy, often just exiting the relationship is the best thing to do. But if you're a kid, and it's your family, you can't. Some people start out trapped. A lot of people start out trapped in something. That can sort of set up a dangerous template in life, where happiness is achieved through escape. That's the association. I guess that's what I was talking about with the rocket ship of the guitar. It was a way—like you were just talking about—to go far away with your body still being right where it is. You can really get completely out of a situation in your mind and in your heart through singing and playing.

Could you go out of body even as a young child, or did that come later?

I think so. I think I did. There's possibility in there, and all kinds of things to be gained. There's also maybe that unhealthy checking out of painful or scary situations so that you can get to the other side. That dissociating, I guess, is definitely one of the skills I came away from childhood with. But making music is different. It's not about checking out. It's not about dissociating, in that same way. When I pick up my instrument, it's really about working through it. It's a very different way of getting to the other side. A more grounded way.

And then you're offering it as a meal to other people, or as a medicine. I keep calling it that—a medicine—because, for me, and I'm sure it's similar for many who love your music, it was a refuge as I was growing up. It still is a refuge in the storms of life. It's a sound space for me. And I think that it must be like that for so many people who resonate so deeply with your music and came up on it as well. It helps wash through heavy feelings and clear unwelcome, stagnant, or negative energy. Was it like this for you when you were young? Would you sometimes feel imprinted with unwelcome energy and then, when you would go into the space and play your guitar, it would help you move it through and away from your energy field?

Yeah, for sure. Definitely. That's it, exactly. I feel extra lucky to have met the guitar. Music does this for so many people. It's such a powerful medium, and I think many of us have that relationship with it. It's like a food-medicine combo that heals us and nourishes us. Music came into my childhood and sort of saved me from whatever—washing through the poison and saving me from sort of starving. Plus, it was not just something I could listen to, but something I could do. It came in the form of an activity into my life, not just in the form of something that I could listen to and appreciate from somebody else doing it. I actually don't remember listening to a lot of music on recordings as a child, but as soon as I got the guitar, I started making music. I had that friend Michael [Ani's guitar teacher and mentor] who I made music with, and so I think it was extra healing for me, because it really does let you bring up and out the struggle that's in you. You get to listen to music and do music at the same time, so it's extra, extra powerful healing.

Did spirit come to you as a child, and were you conscious of it that way?

I was not conscious of it that way, no. But I do think I was tuned in, in my way. Like you said, I was definitely tuned in to the people and the beings around me and what was behind the facades. What were the intentions? What were the feelings and the thoughts? I have read and heard more recently in life that, when you're sort of unsafe as a child, that's a skill that many children learn. You have to be able to read minds because you have to see things coming, and you have to know what the safety level of a situation and a moment is. That was definitely an aspect for me—learning how to read minds.

I know you said that your parents were civic-engagement people, but they weren't churchgoing people, except for once a year. So, the dogma of the church wasn't really a big part of your youth?

Right.

Did they talk to you about God, angels, and demons, or things like that? Was there any sort of rubric that they talked to you about, or was that not really of interest to them?

No, I think they looked at that as a load of crap [*laughs*]. I think they thought that the value of church is community, and I pretty much agree.

Did they talk at all about spiritual things—nondogmatic spiritual stuff?

Oh yeah. I remember when my mom was around the age I am now, when she was fifty or so, she started listening to Ram Dass. I just remember Ram Dass was a big influence on her. I think it was when she got to the age where she started contemplating her own mortality, maybe, and trying to finally achieve some sort of inner peace. I think my mom was even less at peace at fifty than I am, and I still have a lot of work to do. I remember my mom and one of my favorite cousins, Haj, who is a dear friend of hers—they were the same generation—they would swap Ram Dass tapes and talks, and they would have a lot of spiritual conversations.

My mother's a big reader. She's very voracious and reads a lot, and I think she has been on a spiritual quest that's all her own. So, I listened to Ram Dass when I was a kid, as a byproduct.

Did you get into meditating at any point?

No, I've only recently started even trying. I'm just so antsy. Even as I get more exhausted! Antsy and exhausted. A charming combination.

Making music is probably like meditation, though, right?

Yeah, right. I think, in a lot of ways, that is exactly it. It's a meditative state that I get into with music, and it does serve a similar function of freeing my mind from thought and allowing a deeper presence to filter through the noise.

I would describe it as being fully connected. I am lucky to enter spaces through music where I feel totally connected. And again, I feel like I can't necessarily dictate that happening. I'm not in control, in the sense of being able to connect on demand. I just have to start making music. And then, sometimes, even though my hands and my mouth are moving, my spirit goes, *Oh, whoa*, because I feel it quietly connect.

And sometimes you'll be a witness to yourself when you're playing, and then, other times, you'll go out entirely? Is that right?

The experience is much more that I'm standing here singing and playing guitar, and I can hear myself singing and playing guitar, and that's what's happening on a very perceivable level. But sometimes, something that's much harder to define or describe starts happening, and it's not something I'm doing so much as something that the music has made space for, that shows itself. I just experience it along with others, if there's anybody else in the room. Sometimes there's nobody else in the room, and it's just mine alone to experience. But it's a thing that, of course, we all know when we feel it—when a singer taps in, when a musician taps in. It's [almost] imperceptibly different. It looks like the same thing on the surface, but it's more. That's the only way I can describe it.

And then you'll come back and not necessarily recall everything?

Yeah.

It reminds me of how Prince talked about his experiences in an interview included at the end of his memoir [The Beautiful Ones, *released in 2019], which was published after he transcended to spirit. He talked about how he would get to this timeless space in playing where he would see all past, present, and future songs. He would get to this place where he would feel that he would bear witness to everything, and it was an out-of-body experience. And he said that's what all the practicing and rehearsing over the many hours and many years would bring—the ability to get to that point, or the ability to get there more frequently. Do you experience a space beyond time through the music—maybe a place of all that is, including pure potentiality, where there is a sense of perfection or totality to it?*

For me, entering that space when I'm writing, creating a song, it feels sort of clairvoyant, which, in a sense, it is. I think we are all clairvoyant on some level. If you can clear away whatever is the distraction, whatever story is in the forefront, you can know things on many levels, such as the future. Many people do. Sometimes super clearly, like, "That car is going to run into that other car, *boom*." Other times, it is more atmospherically knowing what's coming. That's what it's like for me. I definitely just had to have that experience repeatedly—of being sort of clairvoyant in my songs—to believe in it. Whenever the thing in the song sort of happens, or the thing in the song comes true, or it all becomes clear later what *that* thing meant, *why* that thing, it feels sort of spooky. Or it did feel spooky at first, until I learned about how linear time is really an illusion, born of living in a body.

Like with your Reprieve *album [2006], right? I heard you say somewhere, on a recording, that you felt that some of the songs were anticipating your birthing a child before you realized you would be having a child in the near future. I think it was an interview you did at the 92nd Street Y in New York City.*

Oh, maybe. I don't even remember. That's funny. Sure, I believe myself! [*Laughs*] My first kid was technically an accident, but yeah, exactly. There are so many of those moments that show me, *Oh, right. Time is an illusion.* So, when you're tapping in, you have access to a place that's not of time. I mean, none of us are really of time. That's the kicker. We are only perceiving it on that level, mostly. But there are other levels of perception that many people get to, in many different ways. And definitely, going into that space of creating art is a place for me to access, every now and then, that other level.

Is it like that for your poems, too?

Yeah, maybe. It's funny, my initial feeling when you were asking was no, not really. Because there's something about the guitar in hand that calls, that enables the meditative state. With the poem, though, I feel like it starts from a line or an idea that attaches itself to words and that initial seed comes out of an empty space. I'll be walking, or I'll be gardening, or I'll be driving, and the seed of the poem appears. So I think in that sense, yes. But then, there's something about actually writing with a pen, or just engaging with the page. I don't feel like I have as much out-of-body, out-of-time experience with that activity.

Do you sometimes see apparitions in a kind of empty space, or elsewhere? Energy forms representing spirit, things like that?

I don't really see them. I wish I did. I wish I was more tapped into that. But no, I don't really see them.

Do you ever see, say, plasma-like energy—for example, if you're playing guitar?

No, I want to! Teach me! [*Laughs*]

Maybe we should have a whole retreat in silence and ask that the book simply be revealed to us as a tablet [laughs]. *I sometimes visually sense spirit in sparks of light. One practice that facilitates it is when I stare at one object for some time and still my mind, and let my gaze gradually soften. The object in focus could be anything—a Buddha statue, a painting, an imaginary dot on a blank wall. In general, I'll gradually see spirit, especially in my peripheral vision. In fact, right before I brought up the focus-and-periphery point, some of your lyrics from "32 Flavors" [from the 1995 album* Not a Pretty Girl] *started streaming into my mind:*

> squint your eyes and look closer
> i'm not between you and your ambition
> i am a poster girl with no poster
> i'm 32 flavors and then some
> and i'm beyond your peripheral vision
> so you might wanna turn your head
> cuz someday you might find you are starving
> eating all of the words that you said . . .

The arrival of your lyrics in my mind wasn't, for me, just a fortuitous association. It felt like guidance to remind me to make a point about peripheral vision, as it's so key for how I see aspects of the numinous or spiritual realms. I also feel that the truth of things, including spiritual things, is so often in our peripheral vision, and if we're not consciously aware and expansive in our receptivity, we can miss things.

Mmm, that's cool. I don't have those experiences visually, but maybe I have something similar with sound. Like, in those ways that I was talking about, where I can sort of hear spirit enter the room. The information comes through my ears, but it is not necessarily sound. I feel like I do that just in conversation, too. On one level, I can hear the literal sounds or words being said, but then, on another level, I hear a peripheral transmission. Often, the words are very different from what is coming through on that level. The words can be misleading.

I don't mean to imply that I just pick up on the hypocrisy of the world around me. I pick up on it even when the words are coming from me. In fact, I feel like I'm hypervigilant on that front. But I think maybe, just like we have peripheral vision, we can have peripheral *hearing*. Not just the awareness of a distant sound or a sound off to the side, but the awareness of spirit moving in the background, that you just pick up on. I agree that we are talking about peripheral in terms of attention. Those spaces exterior to the focus of our minds and thoughts, at any given moment. Those are the spaces that seem to leave the most room for spirit to move.

I'm wondering now if that's why I've always been so enamored of the spaces in music. There is as much being communicated there. It's not just in the sounds. A young musician usually makes more sounds—notes, beats, whatever—you can hear them speaking out and listening to themselves talk. Mature musicians tend to play less and listen to the world around them more. You can hear them listening in. And everything *not played* makes room for spirit. I love the deepening conversation of it, too. With Terence [Higgins] and Todd [Sickafoose], I've been playing with them for ten and twenty years, respectively. And the space we create when we play, along with the rest of the relationship, has deepened over time.

Chapter 3

Gut-Brain vs. Head-Brain: How to Honor Our Intuition

In our next conversation, Ani and I unraveled and explored more of the movements and pieces from her broad body of works that illuminate spirit and intuition. We returned to modes of creation and the subtler aspects of tapping in to cocreate with spirit. She spoke further about the heavily produced, committee-led creative approaches to mainstream music, weighing their possible downsides against the positive power and potential of crowdsourcing ideas. In turn, she shared more about her own practice of going inward, into a quiet space, to summon her intuitive powers and serve as a conduit.

Ani spoke of the most powerful spiritual visitation she ever had, from her father as he was transitioning into spirit. She only realized it was him in retrospect, but her father brought her a profound sense of peace and wholeness. This spiritual experience has become a resource for Ani to tap into whenever she fears death. She also reflected upon the role that her father's presence still plays in her life.

We talked about gut instinct, which Ani sees as an inadequately understood, underappreciated aspect of human intelligence across conventional contemporary culture. Her gut-brain guides her through things, ranging from discerning the essence of a song or poem, to navigating the world around her. She believes that if people were to use the word "brain" in reference to the gut as well as the head, then the human experience, and the way forward, might be more easily understood.

In a previous conversation, you mentioned that you feel like you interact with beings that are not human. I was wondering if you could share more about that.

Oh, just paying attention. Just dialing in and noticing them. It seems like so many humans—I mean, humans are bizarre—but yes, so many humans don't even seem to see many *other* humans in their full sentience, let alone other kinds of life forms. It's weird how disconnected we are. Well, not so weird, I guess, if you look at the modern world and how it works. But yeah, I think just slowing down enough to pay attention to another being who is operating in a very different way can help me to connect with them. And practicing empathy. Empathy is a thing that improves with practice. The more I imagine myself as that bug trying to climb that wall, or that plant reaching for the sun, the more I can connect with what their experience is about in that moment.

Do you see things in your mind's eye clearly as visions?

I don't know if I do. I feel like I wish I did more. I'm aware that so much more is possible. You talk about connecting with spirits and seeing them and hearing their voices. I wish I did. I feel like I'm mostly just sitting over here going, "Come on, show me! Help!" [*Laughs*]

Yeah, it's like tuning into a radio signal or something. And sometimes it's fuzzy, and sometimes it's crystal clear if I just turn my proverbial dial. I don't know. It also has to do with the atmosphere for me, whether I'm distracted outwardly and all that. Are there specific moments that stick out to you from when you were interacting with spirit that you want to share, from any time in your life?

Well, I would say that the most profound is when my dad crossed over, when he died, and he came to me in spirit. I would say just *as* he was transitioning and after he transitioned. That was really, really palpable and real. That was probably my only interaction with spirit that was super unmistakable.

Did he appear as a visual apparition, or you just felt him as a presence, or both?

Presence. I guess, at the time, I didn't understand it. I didn't understand at all. I didn't know it was him, and I didn't know that he had died. It was only the next day that I learned what happened. It was just that something hit me really hard, like a wave of feeling that stopped me in my tracks. It was like a sudden wave of resounding calm and peace crashing over me and transforming my way of being. If I think back to the words that came with it, they were, *Everything is perfect, and there's nothing to do. You don't have to do anything. There's nothing to be done.* I stopped all the manic things I was doing and just went to sleep. But I didn't know until afterward that that was my dad who brought that feeling and reassurance and sense of total peace to me. He and I were very connected, very close, and so, I think, the moment he died, he came to show it to me, to let me experience it with him. To reassure me, in some sense. It was the most beautiful, blissful release.

Was that the first time that you felt awash with a profound, total peace in that way?

It's quite probable that I never felt that level of peace, before or since. It was a very striking shift. There was nothing one could see that happened in the room, but something overtook the way I was thinking and feeling and brought me to a uniquely peaceful place.

Do you still tap into that regularly for your writing?

I remember that experience if ever I feel fear or resistance toward death, because that experience was quite vivid about what death is. It's quite beautiful. I feel very grateful to my dad for many things. I feel like that was sort of his last huge gift to me, to show me, *Don't be afraid.* In terms of being creative, I don't think I go back to that experience as a way into being creative. I just get into my work, and I think—yeah, sometimes I do achieve maybe an altered state, but it's not necessarily related to that experience.

As you were telling me about that experience with the spirit of your father, your "Hearse" song [from the ¿Which Side Are You On? album, released in 2012] started playing in my mind. Specifically, it was the line, "i don't want to strive for nothing anymore . . ." For me, that song carries that sort of peace, a deep serenity with all that is. I was just wondering if it was written from a similar kind of space. I always heard the song as being about your husband because you mention the baby in the next room.

Well, that's interesting that you say that, because that song did get written not long after my dad passed. There was a cascade of changes that occurred in my life after he died. I met my fella, and we had a kid. I guess I would say that, in my lifespan so far, being pregnant with my first child and then her early years—maybe the first one or two—were probably the most consistently peaceful times for me. So that would make sense that that feeling would come through that song in particular—and through my songs of that time.

I had another kid six years later, and it was a very different experience. Completely agitating [*laughs*]. When he was inside of me, it was completely agitating for everyone. And then, when he came out, same thing: just hellfire, screaming, total agitation for years. But my daughter was totally the opposite. She's a very chill person, and when she was a part of me, we inhabited a very chill state together.

Did that influence her name, Petah?

Well, I don't know. She's sort of named after the sculptor Petah

Coyne. My partner and I went to an art exhibit of Petah Coyne's work when I was really pregnant, and it's funny because the art exhibit was called *Above and Beneath the Skin*. Petah Coyne uses a lot of natural materials, flowers, even taxidermy animals. Sticks, natural things. And she dips them in wax a lot. She makes these huge sprawling pieces—like, it will cover a whole huge wall, or a big chandelier of wax-dipped flowers. My partner and I loved the art, and we both thought Petah was a cool name, so we ended up naming the baby after her.

And your son, Dante, is he named after Dante Alighieri?

He's named after my dad. Dante is my dad's name. The naming of both of my kids was a very intuitive thing. I didn't even know that my second baby was gonna be a boy until he came out, but I was set on Dante, either way. I just became sure, somewhere along the line, that I wanted to name this baby Dante. And Nappy [Ani's husband] suggested that we could do that even if it was a girl, so that became the plan. And I thought, *Well, this is going to be weird if it's a girl.* We were telling Petah, who was six at the time, and she was so unimpressed with the idea of naming a girl Dante. She was like, "That's not okay." I was like, "Yeah, I don't know. You might be right" [*laughs*]. And yeah—

Do you still feel your father's—oh, excuse me . . .

I was going to answer your question before even hearing it! Yeah, definitely. I feel my dad's presence in that kid. After my dad died, for years maybe, I felt like I had more of a connection with the spirit realm, through my dad. I felt like we were still having conversations. I guess it would've been in dreams, mostly. But I felt like our relationship was continuing. And then, at some point, I felt like somehow that kind of went away. I stopped feeling so connected to him or like the conversation was continuing. I thought that maybe that's just what happens. A person fades away.

But this year, my son is about to turn ten, and I was talking to someone, and I just suddenly realized, *Oh, right! This kid named Dante! That's where my dad's been!* For a long time, I was like, *Where did he go?* And then, just this year, it hit me, *Oh! Duh! He's been right here with me. I've been playing cards with him.* My son reminds me of my dad. Or, at least, our relationship reminds me of the relationship between me and my dad. Our relationship is so much one of total unconditional love. And we just *get* each other. I really do feel like, after about nine years, my dad came back to me. In the physical realm.

Have you shared that with your son?

I'm not sure if I've said that exactly, "Oh, you're my dad!" [*Laughs*]

So, it's the same soul reincarnated for you?

Yeah, well, I kind of suspect that's what's happening. At least, in some aspect.

What year did your father go back to spirit?

I was around thirty-five, so 2004 or 2005.

So, a year or two before Petah was born?

Yeah, and then Dante wasn't born until 2013.

Changing subjects, this is something that keeps coming back to me. You talk about entering into an altered state of consciousness for some of your songs, and it's like you open to receive in a moment of alignment. I know that you said that it's not like you can just call that forth on command. It just happens sometimes. Could you give an example of one of the songs that has arrived in that way?

Let's see if I can pinpoint which ones feel like that in my memory. I have a pretty comprehensive song list right here, so maybe if I just look at it really quick . . . I think "32 Flavors" is like that. I mean, there are so many like that. That's just the one that's on the top of this page! I think there are a lot of them that are like that—especially from back in the day, when stuff was just really flowing. Most of them have some element of that. It would probably be easier to pull out songs that have a different nature, where I'm thinking more or working more with my left brain and involving my thinking. But even with those, before the thinking and the work of it, there's this moment when the spark for the song appears. It doesn't come fully created, there's a lot of real-world ditchdigging involved, but the idea of, *I think I should dig here*, comes.

Do you sometimes wake up out of your trance, and you've written down or recorded most of the music or lyrics to a song?

Yeah, I try to be organized and write out chord charts and write out the lyrics in a legible way, after the initial download. Or I make a little recording of an initial sketch of a vibe I have going, so if I get torn away, it's not just lost. Often, when I'm creating something, things are crossed out, and it's a jumble. One verse is written sideways and goes around the page and then it gets all twisted. It can be hard to figure out later, even for me. I've learned that, years later, to go back and try to relearn a song, if I don't document things coherently soon afterward, they can be impossible to recover. Even a recording, well, it *can* be useful, but it's not necessarily enough. I just have to try to remember what the chords were, but if I write down chord charts, if I chart it—I have a system that I use to document chords and tunings—the probability of being able to revisit things goes up. I've gotten a little better at saying to myself, in the moment, *You're not going to always remember this. Write it down, write it down, write it down*. It's like the boring office work of my one-woman industry.

And songs will come sometimes unbidden? You'll just start hearing a melody in something or on top of something, or in your head?

Yeah. Recording devices can help preserve those moments for future reference. I used to have a little cassette dictating thing. And, of course, now there's the phone. When I'm messing with a song and writing, I use the recording device to help me pick up on a melody or vibe that just went by, in the river. Because I might sing a lot of things when I'm exploring, and not necessarily know what works. Or if I'm coming up with a song in my hands, on the guitar, I may try a lot of different things, in the course of honing in. Because it's so extemporaneous, I can't remember all the proto-versions or attempts that go by, necessarily. Sometimes I'll listen back and go, *Oh, that little melodic thing right there. That's it.* I think it's important to be able to sing and play without thinking or examining it for long periods. At least initially. There's plenty of time to examine oneself and be examined later [*laughs*].

Sometimes it's just the vibe, too, because as you work on something, you can drift away from the initial vibe or energy behind it. Without knowing it, you just kind of mutate. There's a song I'm working on now, and I think it got faster and a little more driving, and then I listened to the first recording I made while working on it and was like, *Oh, right. No. I've strayed from the essence.*

When you are going to different ranges or different iterations of the song or pieces of the melody that you're writing, do you get intuitive vibes or signs when you've hit the essence of the song? Do you get things that are like energy signals on your body or things pinging your intuitive gut sense, or do you see confirmation of sparks around you? I know people get intuitive confirmations in all sorts of ways when they're on to the essence of a song or something else they are creating.

Yeah, gut, for sure. It just feels right in my gut. People still talk about the head-brain as the only brain, but I think that's a super old-school way of thinking about intelligence. And there's the mind-body dichotomy that people are still talking about, which is a bit remedial [*laughs*].

I agree.

Yes, I definitely think that there's more than even a lot of scientists acknowledge about this gut feeling and gut sense—"using your gut," and, "your gut told you." Guts even look like brains. And there are so many nerve endings there. It really is comparable. With the head-brain, the left side has been dominant now for so many centuries. We're not only prioritizing the head-brain in the modern world, but *one side* of it. The left side of the head-brain is kind of in control of everything all the time. It's terrifying [*laughs*].

Basically, I believe the more feminine, right side of our brains has been subordinated by the more masculine left side—with its powers of logic, linear thinking, and language. The other side of the head-brain, the right side, is more involved with awareness and being closely in dialogue with the gut-brain. I think of those centers of intelligence as being more on the feminine spectrum.

I can't help but wonder—because the gut-brain is so interactive—there are so many beings living there and informing the whole, and new perspectives are coming in all the time into the space. Communicating with each other. The gut-brain is getting constant input from the world in a way that, I think, the more isolated head-brain is not. I think that the gut-brain is more in touch. It, quite literally, is more directly in touch with the world around it. I think a general opening of our awareness to the messages from our gut-brains—and a quieting of the narratives of our left hemispheres—is really, really important in this world.

With the gut-brain, you were highlighting how it's receiving many different beings and energies. Do you think about it like a receiving device? Does it have, say, an antenna, metaphorically speaking, that can pick up signals from nature and spirit?

I guess I was thinking most essentially about eating and drinking [*laughs*]. But yes, with these actions, you are literally putting into the gut many, many beings. And the spirits of the plants and animals themselves, their energy and power come in. And the input of the bacteria and the viruses, all of this stuff that you're putting into your gut all the time is bringing all of this knowledge and experience and wisdom with it.

So, like any metropolis, the gut becomes a center of culture and knowledge. There is a synergy that happens with that level of interaction. An exponential intelligence. As with the macro, so with the micro. My mom was an architect and an urban planner, and she showed me how cities are like the brains of human society. Cities are the most densely packed interactive system of diversified intelligence. All these people come together, and they make more than the sum of their parts. When they come together, they inform and influence each other. They teach each other things, and what you get is evolution. You get art. You get culture. You get everything that is inspired and transcendent. Like a city, there's a real diversity at work in the gut-brain, and I think that makes it less myopic. The head-brain is, quite famously, operating more in isolation.

I was just thinking about how you say that songs are like children. I was wondering if there was something to that that is related to the gut-brain intelligence as well, having to do with some songs being born with vitality and a purpose of their own, as people are. I wonder if the songs can be said primarily to emanate from the gut intelligence. Or maybe it depends on the song.

Yes. That's a good way of putting it. I think my songs come from the gut. Sometimes, on their way out, the head gets involved, more so sometimes than at others, but I definitely defer to the gut. Maybe that's why I'm such a purist! Or why I'm such an advocate of art for art's sake. The more thinking that gets involved, the less I trust it [*laughs*].

Like Quincy Jones with Michael Jackson, or George Martin with the Beatles—a producer *can* have what it takes to enter the flow of an artist and amplify them more than homogenize them. And maybe that really *is* the ultimate. The ultimate power of human synergy. But it's subtle stuff, too, because not many collaborations are happening on that level. And, of course, once you've crafted a pristine pop triumph, people aren't left going, "Yeah, but have I lost some elusive and ethereal quality of specificity?" [*Laughs*] No. They're not. They're going, "Fuck yeah!"

I guess I just lean toward art that is quirkier and more specific to somebody or some moment. With the jazz masters, it's about the specificity of a moment. Maybe I fear for that specificity, in a sense, in this world of AI and gene splicing. This world where everything is editable and refinable, what happens to the natural, unrefined world? We just go further and further into the abstractions of our own narratives and preferences and ideas, and we leave nature behind. Anyway, as you can probably tell, I favor the—not necessarily what's most effective in art—but also, yeah, the vitality of the first stroke. The experience, not of perfection, but of being in the room with someone. But maybe that's just my own defense mechanism talking! Or a needless justification for a preference.

You mentioned that some songs are born with a purpose, like people, and I imagine that the particular purpose could get distorted or go out of focus or be flattened, if not erased, if the song is run through a many-layered process. I don't mean to say at all the collective approach is fake or falsifying, but perhaps it involves a sort of laminating or glossing or burnishing or sheening or exfoliating. I mean, those are uncharitable ways of putting it, but I guess just manipulation is another way of saying it. Taking one thing, and then making it seem—or be—more palatable to masses of people. Maybe there's a soul-flattening dimension to that process.

Right, yeah. Making everything more impactful and sound cooler is one way to go, but then also letting a thing be less impactful, like a tiny wild strawberry—less impactful but more indigenous—there is something to be said for that, too. Not refining and engineering every phrase. Letting some moments be awkward, or pick up steam over time, or even drift in and out of focus. Letting something stand as it is. Really real to a moment. When music goes too far in the other direction, into the realm of perfection or whatever, I just wanna kill myself! [*Laughs*] I experience it as more numbing than stimulating. It starts to feel like, not another kind of music, but like the opposite of music. Maybe I am just a vulnerable person who wants the rest of the world to be vulnerable, too [*laughs*]. How many things are ever just one thing?

Yeah, I was just thinking of when you were talking about the feminine and masculine principles being in resonance in great art. You were talking about how there's this linear craft that the artist hones, with all this practicing and mastering. Then, at a certain point, the intuition kicks in and takes the art in another direction entirely, one that renders it transcendent. You mentioned John Coltrane's journeys as an example. I'm wondering if the from-the-gut songwriting process allows for that—what I would call spiritual transmission—to come through more authentically because it's more direct and it's not modulated in the same way.

Yeah, that's a more concise way of putting it [*laughs*].

It's almost like it's a more direct channeling without a filter or a subsequent edit. Another thing that occurs to me is the way you spoke about your voice and the tones, and how the tone is just to be accepted, and how the tones shift with moods, including moods that are so deep you don't know that you're having them. With this kind of hyper-burnishing and polishing of the pop machinery, it seems like it all would sometimes ride roughshod over what I'm calling the tones of the soul without even realizing it, necessarily. And then, maybe, the song loses the authenticity of whatever is coming through to be expressed through the creator, the artist, as a singular soul. And with the tones, you said they're just to be accepted. They're not to be manipulated or even necessarily understood. They're just to be felt and accepted. I wonder, if you had the second order—or the third order or fourth order—production process with other people involved, if that might tamper with the soul transmission or the spiritual essence of the tone that's being expressed.

Yeah, it seems to me like it can't *not* happen, in that kind of process. I mean, how can anybody make a new poem or a new song, anyway? After thousands of years of humanity, what new thing is there to be said? Or new note to be sung? The new things are in the subtle nuances and the minute fluctuations, I think—the exact words that somebody chose—the exact words in the exact rhythm. But, I guess, there is also something to be said for the committee. When a committee is involved, you can have that synergy. As in the gut.

I'm certainly all about crowdsourced intelligence when it comes to government.

As we were talking about this intuitive dimension, I was wondering if it relates to your thoughts on the Great Mother, the light and the dark, and the binaries beyond patriarchal logic. In your memoir, you wrote in one of the chapters about the Great Mother, and you asked her, "Why must it be this way?" And She said, "Everything with you humans is so simple, but in the center of the light is dark, and in the center of the dark is a light." Something to that effect. Is that line from something in particular, or did the Goddess directly say that to you?

I think I've been aware of the yin/yang symbol since I was a kid, and I didn't think a lot about it. But as I got older, I was like, *Oh, whoa, that's a depiction of everything—the whole universe—in one symbol.* It suddenly seemed like the most meaningful symbol a human being has ever drawn [*laughs*]. You know? In that simple drawing is an explanation of how the world works—how everything is in motion, how energy is moving between opposites, and how each opposite, in its extreme, sort of becomes the other. And how, deep in the core of a thing, maybe way beneath where you can see, often lies its opposite.

That's why I go on so much about binaries. Maybe I would be better off just conceding to the antibinary crowd, but I just can't bring myself to do it. The crowd has accepted this, I think, really erroneous idea of what a binary system looks like—and how it functions and what, essentially, it means. There's all this antibinary sentiment, even a flat-out denial, when really, all we need to be doing here is rejecting the man-made abstraction of either/or.

I believe we can observe that existence is an exchange of energy, and that the only way things exist, on the physical plane, is in relationship to each other. We can observe that natural binary systems look like 3D yin/yang symbols, not like a two-dimensional plane with a line going down the middle, and black on one side and white on the other. I don't think we're going to get very far denying the essential binary dynamic in nature. We just need to understand binaries, not in terms of either/or but in terms of the phenomena of interaction.

I have this song called "The Atom" [from the *Red Letter Year* album, released in 2008], which is sort of part hymn to nature and part antinuclear diatribe [*laughs*]. But it's also, at its core, a call for people to venerate the atomic structure as the voice of God. It's a call to really pay heed to the gospels of relationship and balance. We should listen to nature and try to learn from it, not keep fucking with it and trying to control it. Look at what happens when you mess with the fundamental structure of the atom! That is truly the height of destruction and toxicity. I truly believe it's one of the most arrogant, misguided things people can do.

I actually have a forebear, a guy in my family, who worked on the Manhattan Project. He helped invent the atomic bomb, and he got a Nobel Prize for it. But for me, his action, and that of Oppenheimer, is a great tragedy—emblematic of all that is wrong with our world—not a great achievement. And how did Oppenheimer and my great uncle and all those dudes go so absolutely wrong? By ignoring their gut. By ignoring all the misgivings of their feminine centers of intelligence.

I maintain that the only reason spirit ever embodies in the first place is to be able to interact with itself. That, to my mind, is where this whole panoply of binary phenomena comes from. Spirit only leaves the perfection of oneness and splits into two for one purpose—to interact with itself. And through interaction, evolve.

Chapter 4

Telepathy, Feminism, and the Music Industry

The intuition and telepathy that have been with Ani since she was a child have never abated. She has continued to cherish and nourish them throughout her art and life. It is only her consciousness of them that has shifted. In this conversation, we turned to how her telepathic and other intuitive capacities have carried her throughout many critical junctures in her journey. For example, her gut-brain fed her strong aversion to signing to a mainstream record label, despite the enticements people dangled before her and in the face of the serious work of building her own label, Righteous Babe Records. She also shared more about her deep connection to her father and how their ways of communicating beyond ordinary constraints allowed her to have a close relationship with him late in his life, even as his more conventional consciousness was morphing into another way of being.

Ani reflected upon her travels into altered states of consciousness to generate art about trauma, pain, or suffering—and how her fuller view of these works would often open only in retrospect. As she writes these works, she interlaces meanings and memories, the significance of which she may discover decades after the fact. This process may be prolonged or delayed in the case of subject matter that is particularly painful or terrifying.

Ani also related how she found the patriarchal tenets and tacit principles for navigating relationships often difficult, in her youth. She sees this system as setting up young people to fail. Many of the de facto rules in this culture are Christian in nature, she said, and she has drawn upon biblical phrasing in her songs in order to redeploy the words and recast the messages in subversive ways that work to empower women, especially. Through these symbolic reversals and plays on words, she seeks to lay bare many fraught gendered experiences and to throw into high relief the hypocrisies of patriarchal conceptions and practices.

While Ani's songs and poems relate her own experiences, they also serve as prisms for illuminating the contradictions, inequities, and—at times—absurdities within broader cultural consciousness. Her intuition leads as her soul's expression flows in her art, articulating multifaceted commentaries and meanings which continue to unfold across time.

During our last conversation, you were talking a little bit about the years after your dad went to spirit, but before your son Dante was born, and how you would talk to your dad regularly in spirit. Would you want to share any of the ways in which you would connect with him, how you would interact with him?

I would say pretty exclusively it was in dreams. I would meet him in dreams. But the dreams were not memory dreams. It was not like I would dream about the past and things that happened between us when we were together, in human form. I would have new conversations with him in dreams, or I would have new experiences with him. Right now, I can't think of an example, but I remember being aware that, in these new conversations, I was learning new things. I felt very strongly that the conversation between us was continuing. It didn't feel like I would just invent scenes of us that hadn't happened yet, or that we would talk about things I already knew. I felt like I was discovering things through the dream conversations.

I was just thinking of your song "Angry Anymore" [in which Ani sings about her parents and their relationship, released in 1999 on her Up Up Up Up Up *album]. I know you wrote that while he was still alive, but for some reason the feeling of that came to me. Did you ever talk to him about that song before he crossed over into spirit?*

No, no. He had a very long, slow decline. I would say that the last ten years of his life were not ones where he was keeping up on my work and listening to my records and talking with me about present events and things. He was checking out of that level of awareness, and he was separate from that "doing things" level of my life. He was in a nursing home and he increasingly had "dementia." I mean, I put quotes around dementia because my feeling is that the nursing home is—or at least certainly was for him—a numbing, alienating place, disconnected with the rest of life. I imagine maybe there's an example out there of a nursing home that's cool and loving, but that's not really what we're talking about here.

I'm trying to say this matter-of-factly now, without breaking down and sobbing about it—all those years that he was stuck in that environment, just waiting between visits from his loved ones—I think, especially me, as he would come alive maybe most easily with me. My visits were few and far between. I was traveling the globe and working my ass off and completely ensconced in becoming myself. I was rarely even going home to Buffalo. And then, when I would go home, it was emotionally hard to go see him. Part of me wanted to live in denial that he was even living where he was. Going and spending time with him was this excruciating experience on many levels, because then I would leave, and I would leave town again, and it would refresh all of my pain around it. The guilt and the sorrow that I felt for him, et cetera. All this to say that I felt that, as he slipped into dementia, that that was really the sanest thing for him to do. He checked out of his current reality in self-defense. It made total sense to me. I imagine that, in the same circumstance, I would've done the same.

I think I can relate, in my own life, to being trapped in painful circumstances and devising means of psychological escape. I escaped into fantasies, which became art, which became a career. Putting yourself somewhere else is a very necessary thing when where you are is too painful to tolerate.

Even though you would find him in the nursing home, he would think he was at the office thirty years earlier, and that person there was this other person that he knew. He might not know everybody's name or the exact relationship that he had with them—that all became more and more fluid—but for me, staying in this sort of fixed narrative of a concrete reality would've been too excruciating. So, becoming more fluid with it and creating different narratives in his head, which were more interesting and more satisfying, more meaningful—this all made total sense to me. I just wanted to qualify the word dementia with respect to what happened to him, because I think, given the circumstance that he was living in, it is a very ingenious strategy of the brain, and it made for a higher quality of life. Plus, I felt that, even as he would mix up names and dates and facts and figures, that others think of as static or fixed, he was often more emotionally aware and present than some of the other people in the room. Like, people in my family who were not mixed up or checked-out in the conventional sense. I felt like he had the ability to be totally checked-in, emotionally. So, I just want to also recognize that there are different ways of being in touch with reality.

I guess every once in a while—not often—people will talk about dementia and things like that as altered states of consciousness that are akin to what mystical healers or great artists experience—including yourself, perhaps, when you write your songs? And this altered state of consciousness is not necessarily lamented if the person is happy or at peace, and it can be celebrated and recognized as a gift.

Yeah, we're a little bit more ready, although not entirely, to accept this state in children. "Oh, their active imagination." We accept it and even play into it and promote it in children. Like, "Yeah, let's imagine all these things are happening, and there are fairies out there in the woods, and Santa Claus is on your roof." With children, we acknowledge the fluid experiences they're having—like when my daughter tells me she's Cinderella, I don't say, "Oh, you're confused and that's a problem!" I say, "Okay, Cinderella, it's time for dinner" [*laughs*].

Being more fluid and less static with your interpretation of reality is a natural product of unbridled human creativity. And to tell adults that at some point they lose the right to exercise that creativity and have to subscribe only to a collectively determined or sanctioned idea of reality at all times is shutting down part of our nature which ideally would exist all the way through our lives.

I was just thinking that so many people must ask you about your secret sauce or your superpower or what have you—how you do it all. Maybe part of it is that you haven't abdicated this part of yourself that was alive in childhood. You didn't allow it to be shut down completely as you kept traveling. You allowed these altered states of consciousness to come through, and the words to come out as they came out without questioning them, and you followed that as one of the streams of your life. Do you think that this would be accurate to say, and that the telepathy might just be one aspect of that?

Yeah, and I think the reason that I continued to allow it is because I was free to do so, and I was not institutionalized or whatever and told that it was not okay. I was on my own in a lot of ways. But it was not even something I could necessarily control or stop. It was not exactly a choice. Again, when I say I can relate to my dad and his technique for surviving the last decade of his life, it's because when I would go to see him, he would be happy to see me. He wasn't wallowing and being all torn up at the time in between visits. He was happy to see me and could connect in joy with me, and love. I think his dementia was part of preserving a kernel of his soul, his spirit, and keeping it intact for the moments when it could come alive.

And I think I did that too, throughout my childhood. I escaped into fantasy worlds, into my imagination. I danced, I painted, I sang, I played guitar. I did every form of art that I knew of and had access to, because I was escaping the nuts and bolts of my present reality and my unhappy family. The shouting and the fear and the stress and anxiety, the anger that was dripping in the air, the constant apprehension. Or the deep well of sadness—the drinking.

I escaped into my guitar, into my art, into my singing, into my drawing, into my songs, into my head, into my fantasies, into books. It became a very ingrained coping skill. So, when I went out into the world, I carried this skill with me. If you're not super jazzed about where you are, go somewhere else.

Do you think that you kept a part of yourself always sacred and to yourself, close to your heart and not sharing it with people, relating to your imaginative capacities that were sometimes realized in, say, altered states of consciousness—or in what we could call spiritual states of awareness—because people might have psychologized it?

I guess I feel like the closest answer is no. I feel like I put it right out there. I mean, there are choices to be made in art along the way and that choice, every time you make it, is such a tricky one. That choice of how much to show and tell and in what way to expose yourself. Or to expose others. Or risk hurting others with your own truth or your own perspective. So yeah, I guess along the way, sure, there are things that I've left out, right up to and including in the memoir. I'm not going to expose everything. Mostly in deference to other people. But I think that right from the beginning, more so than not, I leaned toward expressing myself and showing myself really openly and honestly. It's almost like it wasn't *for* other people. It wasn't like my focus was, *What am I trying to get across to this other person? What do I want to tell them or show them?* Or, *What do I need to hide from them?* I think the focus was more, *Get this out of my body*. And so, it came out.

I think I was just really immediate with the process of turning my pain or my struggles into art and forms of expression and making something beautiful of it and something exciting to do, and something satisfying. It feels satisfying to move your body in dance. So I would get totally into it, in a way that maybe not a lot of the other kids in the room would. And then, adults would pick up on it, like, "Look at Ani go!" Or, "Look at this poem this little girl wrote." So people started to notice and affirm it, which was encouraging. It pretty quickly became fuel for positive feedback loops with the world. So that's very generative. But I think that, right from the beginning, I wasn't necessarily focused on "the other," struggling with what to say and what not to say. I was focusing on myself and struggling with what was happening internally and trying to heal that.

Gig poster from the Save the Whales and Dolphins benefit (1981).

Guitar teacher and friend Michael Meldrum, from Ani's journals from the 1980s.

Spirit Tribe. *Painting by Ani (2012)*.

Self-Portrait. *Painting by Ani (2011)*.

Family. *Painting by Ani (2006)*.

Over It. *Painting by Ani (2010)*.

Ani's tree shadow drawing from her journal, from the late 1970s.

Ani's rocks, New Orleans, Louisiana.

Ani's rocks under a full moon, New Orleans, Louisiana.

Photograph by Susan Alzner, 2023

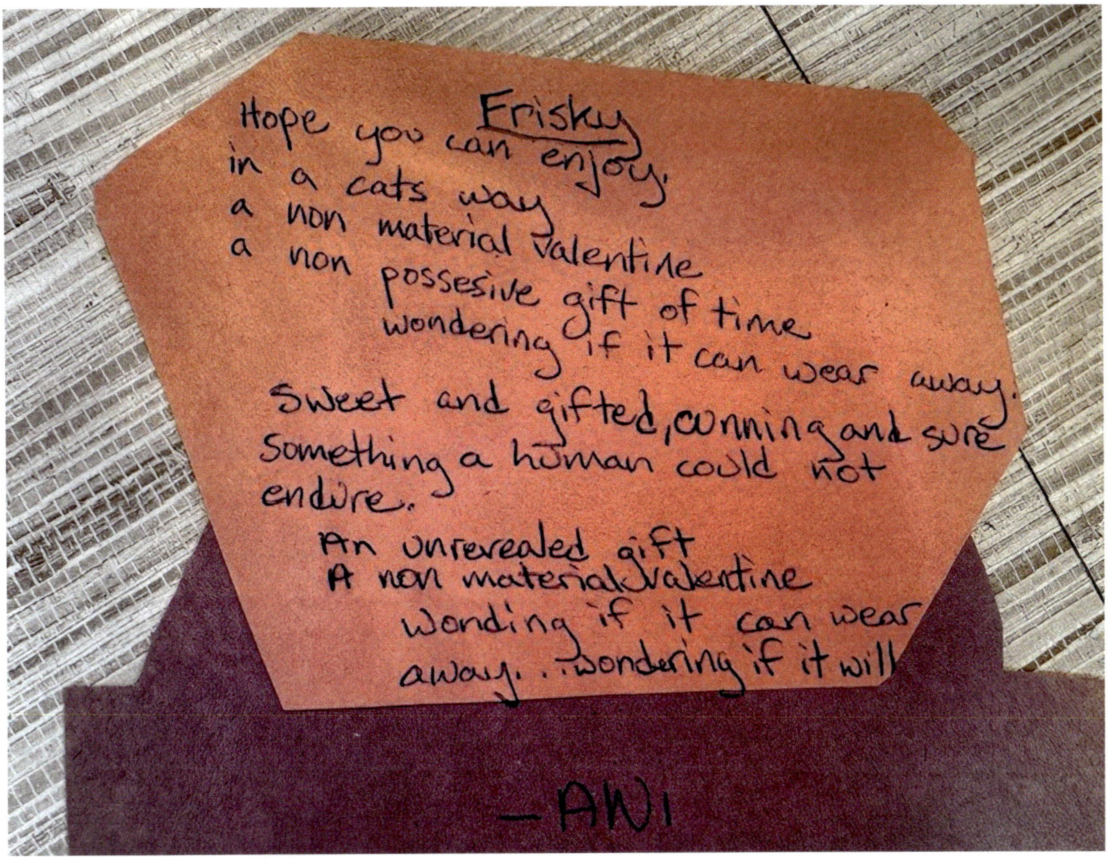
Frisky
Hope you can enjoy,
in a cats way
a non material Valentine
a non possesive gift of time
wondering if it can wear away.
Sweet and gifted, cunning and sure
Something a human could not
endure.
An unrevealed gift
A non material Valentine
wonding if it can wear
away. . wondering if it will
—ANI

Handmade Valentine's Day card from a young Ani to her cat Frisky.

Ani in kindergarten (mid-1970s).

From Ani's personal collection

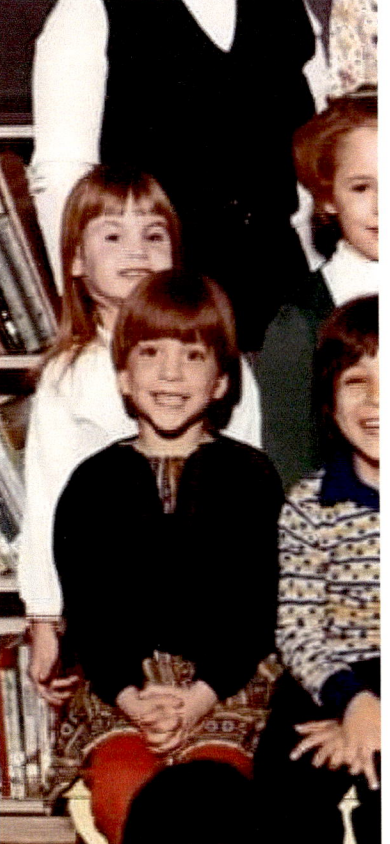

Ani and her father, Dante Di Franco, 1971.

Dante Di Franco (1970s).

From the photo shoot for a cover story in Spin *magazine, 1997. Photographs by Andrew Macpherson.*

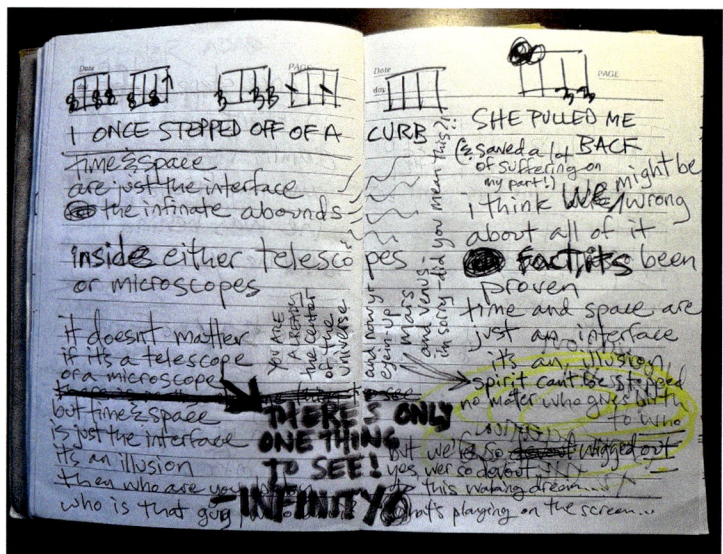

Lyric explorations and chord charts for "Baby Roe," from Ani's journal.

A collection of Ani's writings from the nineties, all on scrap paper.

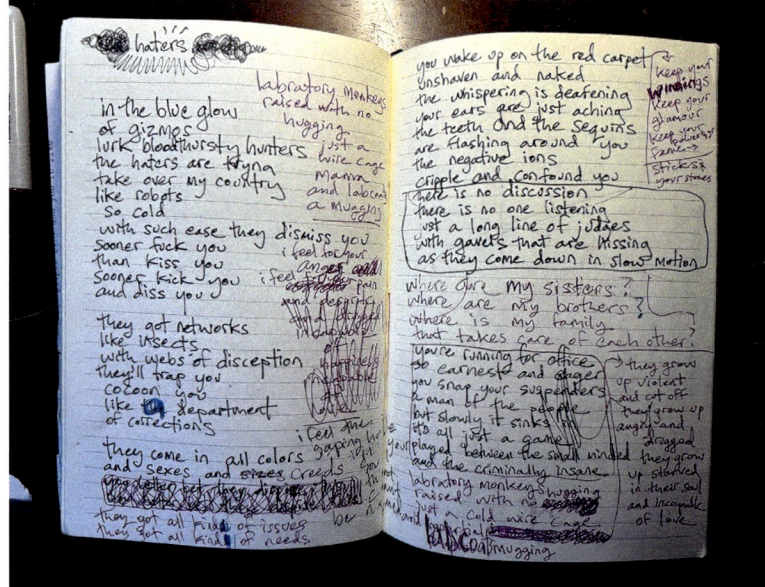

Lyric explorations for the song "Binary," from Ani's journal.

I was just thinking back to your first records as you were speaking, and I absolutely get that sense from them. You just let it all out. Your song "Out of Habit" [from her first album, Ani DiFranco, *released in 1990] just started playing in my mind, as well as "Every State Line" [from the 1992 album* Imperfectly] *and "Hide and Seek" [from the 1997 album* Living in Clip]. *These songs so straightforwardly spoke of pain and things that often people will withhold from others, and sometimes even from themselves, from their own conscious awareness.*

It does feel like powerful catharsis, to hear you play and sing these songs. They are also like an empowerment medicine, which perhaps is almost incidental to the act of getting it out of you and into the song that you're then offering to the world. I think people, especially women, receive that as an empowerment tablet. You're showing that, not only is it okay to talk about this stuff, but it's okay to sing about it on stages in front of large audiences or on records released to the world. Like, next time you're wondering why a woman seems angry or upset, maybe you could check this out.

Yeah, when the #MeToo movement came to the fore, my immediate sensation—I mean, now it's so much a part of the lexicon that I associate it with itself—in the beginning, I had this really strong association with how many times I'd heard those exact words from other women. I was a little ahead of that wave that's thankfully cresting, where women's stories and female perspectives are becoming undeniable in a broader way. I was engaging in the task of calling out the patriarchy in the early nineties, and yeah, just talking about what it's like being a girl, or a young woman, and hearing overwhelmingly from other young women, "Oh my god, thank you, thank you, thank you. Oh my god, *me too*."

You mentioned before that in your childhood you felt like learning to read people—their body language, their thoughts—was a safety mechanism, maybe even first and foremost. Maybe that was part of your inbuilt security system, while making your way in the world as a teenager and getting emancipated, or emancipating yourself, I should say. And then, perhaps this played into your going out in the world as an artist and declining all of these offers from people who were offering you record deals. Instead, you created Righteous Babe Records, and you stayed with that. I'm wondering if there was a deep intuitive aspect to that. Were there, in your gut-brain, alarm bells going off?

Right. I mean, I had a relationship with my gut-brain that was ongoing and close and important, so when I walked into whatever situation—x, y, z—you know, the record company office—the gut was telling me all sorts of things, like it was doing at all times, to keep me safe, from as far back as I could remember.

When it comes to my head-brain, I feel like I am in the habit of processing things twenty years after the fact. I will wait at least that long, sometimes. I think that's sometimes how long it takes to feel like you've exited whatever the situation was and are truly safe. For people who have never been molested or raped, for instance, it's absolutely logical to say, "Well, if she was raped or whatever, why didn't she say anything for twenty or forty years? That seems kind of suspect." If you've never been there, that's a completely logical suspicion. But for those who have experience with the survival technique of suppression—of suppressing something until you're in a safe enough place in your life that you can actually psychologically and physiologically look at it—you understand entirely.

People have literal amnesia of traumatic events because sometimes that's the only way to survive and keep going, psychologically. If you don't have the right support for healing, time is what it may take to get yourself all the way to a safer place, a place where you might be able to let that demon out of its cage and face it. Those survival techniques are very, very common, but not known to everyone or understood by everyone. I believe they may be known, most broadly, by women.

Your "Out of Range" song [on the album of the same name, released in 1994] keeps playing on top of this conversation we're having. I always had a visceral reaction to this song—this sense that the intensity of emotions or ingrained patterns can fade, you just have to drive out of range, so they don't keep holding the same kind of grip over you. And with this deep feeling or reaction to your music, it's not just what you say; it's also the energy that comes through what you're saying. You say it with such truth and conviction. With such power, and in such a straightforward manner: "This is what it is." The truth vibration that cuts through what I call the bullshit chatter in my mind or in my emotional field, even. You write with great conviction of your self-empowerment, yet you are also very vulnerable and open about your ambivalences. Even in "Out of Range," you sing:

> and i try
> to draw the line
> but it ends up running down the middle of me
> most of the time

So, you said that it often takes you about twenty years to start really processing things that have happened. Do you sometimes look back at songs like that—maybe ones that came through you in a semi-altered state—and now they resonate with your processing of things from the past? Do they reveal or disclose things to you that perhaps you didn't fully see or recognize at the time, almost as though your spirit or another consciousness was speaking to you, through you? Do you think your soul was speaking to you about things that you would later come to see, like turning over stones, in a conscious way?

Yeah, I think there was a lot of messaging myself back and forth through time. At the time of the writing, it's not necessarily about consciously processing something. It's more about unlocking the subconscious and finding homeostasis through that release.

Yeah, I was just thinking about trauma, how usually when people narrate trauma or when they give accounts of trauma, it's tricky to fully register it in the so-called secular rationalist legal system, right? Many psychoanalysts or psychologists or others who specialize in understanding trauma will say that the truth—if it comes to the conscious level for the person who suffered the trauma—comes in shards. Temporality is nonlinear in the experiencing, remembering, narrating. The account, if it has veracity, is going to come in jagged bits and parts that don't add up because that's how people can deal with it on a conscious level, with remembering and narrating. It reminds me of what the psychoanalyst Jacques Lacan said, in one of his multitudes of oracular aphorisms: "Every truth has the structure of a fiction" [from his Seminar on the Ethics of Psychoanalysis, Book VII, *12].*

I think that, oftentimes in art, it's not necessarily that it is fictional, but the truth is embedded in these representational forms that may be shard-like, nonlinear, uneven, partial. The art doesn't have to align, necessarily, with so-called real-world facts. For example, I was struck by how you were saying in your memoir that the song "Shameless" [on the Dilate *album, released in 1996] was written from a space of longing for your first husband, before you married, when you were both involved with other people. You sing:*

> i gotta cover my butt cuz i covet
> another man's wife

And I never knew that the song was about a guy because there was that decoy of another person's wife.

I was also just thinking about your writing on difficult things in general. Maybe it's sometimes easier to depict them in fictional or semifictional surface forms, even as you are delivering the truth vibration of it, the authentic essence of a song. In this vein, I thought of your mentor and friend, the poet Sekou Sundiata, who would tell you to forget about the facts and just tell the truth. I remember you said that you drew upon that wisdom in your poems and songs.

Well, if I could just pause for one second, on that song lyric from "Shameless," just to drill down. It wasn't that I was disguising the literal facts of the scenario in a metaphor or, you know, only able to approach the truth in shards. My using that phrase, "coveting another man's wife," is a biblical reference. What I'm doing is I'm trying to talk on many levels about the fact that, in patriarchal religions, adultery is a sin because love and possession are inextricable, and to make matters worse, of course, it's the male who traditionally possesses the female. Within this sort of patriarchal Christian society, there have been a lot of allowances made for the male sex drive and the natural state of polygamy for a male, but not so for the female. So, in that song, I'm not only trying to say that I'm in this tricky situation by being in love or in lust with somebody who has a partner, but that there's almost no way of navigating it well, in a society that sets us up for failure [*laughs*]. I just happen to be writing about all that without letting gender dictate what I can say or how I can say it, or how I can play with metaphor.

I think when we are young, most people are naturally promiscuous—naturally polygamous and exploratory. But we are instantly found in this structure where we have to deny and suppress that. Or compartmentalize it in some way. And then we become villains when we fail to do so. Most people, when they're young, break up with people by cheating on them. It's rarely, you know, *I feel as though I don't want to be monogamous any longer, so I'm going to use my words first and set up a new dynamic, because, of course, these things are very fluid and malleable, and we are free and empowered and equal.* This whole society is built on patriarchal religions which are antigay and antiwoman. The society exists within thought frames that are narrow and specific. So our natural animal sex drives are trying to manifest in impossible situations. That's why I used that biblical phrase, because we're still living, we're still answering—on a daily basis, all of us—to a book that was written by and for straight men, a long time ago. Referencing the Bible is a way of referencing the broader social context in which the whole individual love-triangle thing is happening. And how that context can inhibit creative solutions and understanding, and good outcomes.

I was just thinking about your song "Adam and Eve" [also from Dilate*]. That just started playing in my mind as well. The lines:*

> but i know it's cuz you think you're adam
> and you think i'm eve

It feels like the same kind of thing.

Yeah, I was a little distraught at the time of writing that song [*laughs*], but I think, again, I was trying to push against the whole society based on a book which is, by and large, simply codified patriarchy, to my mind. So again, it's a female trying to say, "I'm not just a character in your story. I have my own story."

And now I'm thinking of your song "The Million You Never Made" [from the album Not a Pretty Girl, *released in 1995]. When you were resisting all these dudes who were trying to get you on their labels or whatever, in their beds or what have you, did you feel that you could read their minds and intentions? Would you get the gut knowledge and then say no to them? I remember from your memoir that you almost signed with a couple guys in the early days in New York, and then you just said no. You just knew. Do you think that was telepathic?*

Yeah, intuitive. The telepathy plays into the intuition. I think just being in touch with: how does something feel in my body? Just feeling that heaviness when I envisioned myself moving into that world of shiny commercial maneuvers—the magazines and the videos and dressing up for the Grammys—not that that's a given or anything, but that was sort of literally what people would say: "I am going to make you a star. We're all going to make tons of money." And I think you don't have to go very far to see that, after that moment, that's exactly what they did. Just not with me.

How do you mean?

It was super hard for me for a bunch of years because people who didn't know when or how I started would ask over and over and over again if Alanis Morissette was an influence on me. Especially outside of the United States. Everyone spoke about me as an offshoot of her, because she was considered one of the first outspoken women—showing her anger in this new way, singing from a female point of view, putting a hand up to a lot of male behavior, this kind of thing—that they'd ever heard. They just didn't happen to be tapped into the subculture I existed in. So they compared me to her, and then to this one, and then that one. It was very humbling to just sit there and say nothing. I would say nothing because it's really not important who came first or whatever, except to our egos, which are really not important at all [*laughs*].

The way capitalism works, if they can't sell you, for whatever reason, they're going to sell something *like* you. Like Elvis Presley selling rhythm and blues. They're going to find the thing to capture and sell because they see a market for something. So they were watching this thing happen around me, and they began to see a market for a new kind of feminist perspective in music, or a queer perspective or whatever. Even people I knew, who cared about me, would say, "This movement is going to get packaged and sold, so are you really going to forego being that guy?" I guess, for me, the answer was yes, because when I pictured trying to operate in and become myself in that music-biz world, I felt a heaviness in my body. I felt aversion. I felt sadness and anger. I felt I could see that future. I could see the ridiculousness of me trying to play that game. And I could see wanting to shoot myself in the head like Kurt Cobain. I could feel in my gut how wrong it would be.

And then, you know, there are other things that, fundamentally, when I'm around political activists who are changing things for the better—when I'm around, you know, my folk community, the "uncool" cultural wing of the Pete Seegers and the Utah Phillips, I feel drawn. I feel inspired, I feel hope. I feel a sense of purpose and of possibility. On a super-simple level, I was working with the binary forces of attraction and aversion. That's what guided me.

You felt like it would be soul-sucking to be in these boxes and forms of contractual obligation with a mainstream record company?

Yeah, like I can choose to surround myself with people who inspire me and feed me energy and inspiration, or who suck it out of me. So, what is it worth?

Chapter 5

The Illusion of Self:
How Ani DiFranco Doesn't Exist

"Ani DiFranco is a shirt," Ani stated, rather matter-of-factly, in this conversation, as she further explored the illusions of self. She returned to reflecting upon her understandings of the ultimate unity of consciousness, as well as the powers of the stories we tell ourselves about ourselves and (so-called) others. She explained how the more masculine left-brain processing often propounds and propagates false identities, comparisons, narrations, and hierarchical value judgments. She connected this left-brain thinking to the prevalent human ego-based preoccupations with being greater than, or less than—or of being "the best" or not being good enough. When we step away from false idealizations, positive or negative, we can begin to recognize the truths in ourselves that our reactions to others have been showing us. This is part of how Ani navigates praise or criticism. She understands all these dynamics as forms of recognition, whether in the valences of attraction or aversion. They indicate things that she is mirroring to people about themselves.

She also reflected upon how the collective policing of speech in the Internet era has amplified the virulence of criticism and the consequences of risk-taking. She opts out of participation in online discourse as much as she can, and she steers clear of debates on social media platforms so that she can remain centered and focused on her life and art.

The Spirit of Ani

Ani shared more about the ways in which her art requires her to attempt to quell ego-level concerns so that she can tap more fully into the essence of relationality and the interconnectedness of all. She understands consciousness to separate itself so that it can relate, experience itself, and expand in various ways. She associates this mode of creating and relating to the world as being informed by the feminine, right-brain perspective and experience. To her mind, all of this is profoundly entwined with the ways in which many women—and feminism itself—prioritize relationships and interrelatedness over individuality or competition.

For Ani, true healing of all individual and societal maladies must start with addressing the problematic nature of patriarchy, in its most profound forms. She explained that, in her understanding, the subduing—or even muting—of the right brain, or gut-brain, intuitive knowing faculties within *all* people, is part and parcel of patriarchy. This disjuncture between right- and left-brain perspectives, along with the quieting or silencing of intuition, harms humanity.

More broadly, Ani interlaced reflections on her reckoning of waking life as an invention. She has lived into an understanding that, in fact, life itself is a dream. An awareness of this oneiric quality of everyday life can give way to liberation, rather than resignation or nihilism. Once someone has a sense of a unified consciousness behind the illusory veils of separate forms, they can more easily relegate ego concerns to the sidelines of thought and tap into the ever-flowing stream of creative existence. This river of vitality births transcendent art and allows for a life of freedom.

Do you want talk about the recurring dream at all, the one you mentioned at the end of your memoir and that appears in its title, No Walls and the Recurring Dream?

I called it a recurring dream, but I think I was using that wording poetically, to mean the recurring dream of my life. It's not that I literally have a recurring dream when I'm sleeping, about this thing that I do now—many nights, many months, many years and decades in a row. It's more like the recurring dream *is* the waking life. That was how I was messing with it, that life itself is a dream. Life is a but a dream [*laughs*].

There's something about that moment that is very poignant for me—where I'm crossing a theater stage in the dark, and it's empty, and there's just the ghost light and the memory of what happened earlier [during a show]. How different the whole space is when it's alive with music and people, and everything that that brings with it. Only hours before, the room was brimming with movement and meaning and energy and emotion, and now, this is all that's here— just quiet and emptiness and stillness. The rest seems like a dream [*laughs*].

I feel that sort of deep nostalgia; even though I'm still living it, I sort of feel like, *Am I alive? Am I dead?* The whole adventure of my life feels like a memory. *Remember what that felt like to be standing together, enveloped in a song, all of us?* Feeling totally connected and engaged with life. To be on the stage late at night, when the place is empty and you're alone, and everyone is gone—it just makes me feel that feeling of, *That part is over.*

That was the recurring dream that I had—that we invented all these ways to find ourselves and each other, and our joy and our purpose. That we actually did all that stuff! And then, you just quietly exit that adventure, and you're off into the unknown.

I thought you were actually having that dream while physically asleep when I read the end of your memoir. So, it's about how life is a stage and a recurring dream?

Yeah, right. So, that's the tradition in theaters. Any theater people will be familiar with the ghost light. It's a longstanding tradition. In old theaters and opera houses, they put out a lamp in the front middle of the stage at night, to keep away the evil spirits or to help the good spirits find their way. They generally put the lamp in the exact position where I was standing during the show, so it calls up the metaphor in me—of my job being related to that of the ghost light.

In these old buildings, where so much art and music and drama or whatever happens—you feel it.

It's still resonating, and the spirits are attracted, I think, to such spaces. There's a lot of spiritual residue. So yeah, the ghost light is a thing, and it's so dramatic at night, especially with the contrast of what was happening only hours earlier—with a room full of people and electricity and emotion and passion and music and reckoning and bonding and becoming. And now it's just this solitary ghost light, there in the dark. And I have this moment, kind of every time, where it seems like a dream, and that feeling feels like a window into this life that I'm having now.

And then you'll fade out sometimes, too, right? So there's a kind of lucid, trancelike state, and then you come back, and it's over?

Yeah. That's what I was looking at, in my recurring dream. That I kept finding myself on the bow of this ship, you know, the ship of performance. It's the endless, seagoing adventure of being a performing artist. And that's what life essentially is, anyway—it's theater.

Do you consciously set an intention when you go onstage to clear the negative energy and help people heal or feel elevated in the space? Or is it just automatic, as that's where the songs are coming from—from a medicinal place?

Automatic. Thankfully, that is a thing that happens when I just try to be honest and present. I think if I'm doing anything mentally before I go on, it's, *Drop the veils, drop the veils. Turn down the ego.* If there's a nervousness, or there's a self-consciousness, or there's a worry, it's like, *Put all that down. Let go of the fear of judgment and open up to something bigger.* I don't have rituals so much that are super defined before I perform. But I like to be alone-ish for enough time that I can center myself and try to let go of whatever might get in the way of me connecting with the song and just offering it without any of those things that impede that process—like, worrying about how my hair looks or how my voice sounds that day, or what people think of me. All that stuff just gets in the way of doing the best art and connecting the most thoroughly. So all I'm trying to do is get myself into the most open, available, unfettered place to perform from. And then all the rest does or doesn't happen on its own.

And with "drop the veils," do you mean that you go into a trance or, say, let your higher self or spirit take over?

I guess I'm thinking of the veils of whatever might be shrouding my ability to be totally available and connected, because I think that's really what it is. I don't have to play all the way right and sing it all the way right. Or show off. I just have to be real, and I have to be present. So the veils for me are what get in the way. It's the ego. Which, for me, usually comes in the form of worry and self-doubt and nervousness. But it's like, why would you be nervous if it doesn't matter? It doesn't matter whether you impress or disappoint or wow or embarrass yourself. What matters is that you show up. Show up for your life while you can. That's the only thing that really matters for any of us. So I want to walk onstage with as little of the ego noise as possible. Where I'm not worrying about what people think of me, I'm free to get right to the point [*laughs*].

And then, once you open up and let down those barriers, then people can join you for the ride through the sonic medicine or soundscape . . . or how do you think of it? Just like a sound space that comes into the physical space with you, and you and others can be held and journey in it?

I think what people really want to see when they go to a show, or what they want to hear when they listen to somebody sing, is that person be free—that person be fully embodied in their own skin. I know I can hear the subtle difference between myself singing when I'm totally free and there's no energy toward, *How do I sound? How am I coming across? I didn't like what just happened there.* You know, when none of that matters. Those are, I think, the best moments of art. I think that those are the most rewarding for both sides of the equation—the singer and the listener. And when you are free and unafraid, you take risks, and that is inspiring for those witnessing it.

In my experience, your authenticity and your vulnerability and your freedom, and your inhabiting it—full force—is certainly shared by other people, but it's also rare and remarkable. And it's something that I really responded to, even as a teenager. I didn't know exactly what it was. And then, I realized, Oh, she's real. She's authentic. I can feel this. Of course, a lot of people have this reaction to your music.

Yeah, I mean, it's super contagious, which is the glorious part, if somebody is free and unafraid. You can feel that, and then you can be that, or you can become that, you know? I mean, a lot of performers, on recordings or onstage, project a super-confidence, and that can be one way of doing it. That's such a great thing to witness and to absorb. *I'm gonna be self-assured, too. I'm gonna strut my stuff.* It's a great feeling to have that model to absorb. What does it look like and what does it feel like when somebody's just like, "Right here, right now, it's going down." *Boom.* We all want to capture that, in some way, in our lives. Maybe it's confidence, being self-possessed—like, if that person can walk out in front of twenty thousand people and strut it and just rock it and make it happen, that leaves me with the feeling that I can do that, too, in my way.

I think with my particular personality, I've never been very confident. I feel like I'm intrepid, but I'm not confident a lot of times, or in a lot of ways. So when I walk onstage, I think my angle on it is not so much, well, whatever—I think I just focus on more of the honesty and the freeing myself from self-doubt—enough to just not care. I try to just prioritize joy and freedom over other people's opinions and stop letting that get in the way, because it's so much more fun to do anything without fear of judgment in the forefront.

I think I'm typical of a lot of women. Just to generalize, men often take fears and anxieties and project them outward, they become aggressive, they become angry. When, really, it's pain or fear. Women easily, of course—we're just talking in generalizations—turn it inward. It looks like sadness, or it might look like self-flagellation—as opposed to other-flagellation. But I've gotten to the age where I'm just sick of hearing myself worry and be nervous before I go onstage, or come off a stage and worry and beat myself up for not doing good enough this, that, the other. I try to tell myself instantly, *Ego, ego, ego. That's all ego talking. Get over it.* Whether it's saying I'm the best or I'm the worst, whether I'm beating up myself or beating up the other, it's all based in fear. Fear of not being good enough. It just gets in the way. It gets in the way of being the best artist, the most effective healer, if you will, or the most effective human being.

We often think of ego as just the manifestation of, *I'm the best.* But I think people who spend so much time and energy, like I have, thinking, *I'm the worst, I'm the worst*—that's all self-absorption, too. That's all just draining your life force into something illusional. It's like, *First of all, who's "I"? Second, what does it matter? Even if I'm the worst, who cares?* It's like, *Get over it. Think about something meaningful* [laughs]. I try to. Mostly, my struggle as a performer is to refocus away from my ego, long enough to do anything well.

Do you think of the ego as a separate space, or an illusion of a separate space, within you? Like it speaks its own language, does its own thing?

Yeah. I think I'm pretty intellectually aware, and I also have had glimmerings of real experience, with the fact that Ani DiFranco is an illusion—it's a shirt [laughs]. It's just a shirt that spirit is wearing. It's one shirt made into a lot of other shirts at the merch table that support my whole game. But seriously, the whole thing is a shirt because the idea of myself as even truly separate from you is the big illusion. It's because we're inhabiting these different bodies temporarily and interacting with each other, we think of ourselves as separate.

Doesn't mean I'm not Ani DiFranco, for the record! [Laughs]

No, seriously. And I'm Lauren. Yeah, I think the only way to really leave this—*Am I better than you? Am I worse than you? Am I okay? Am I good enough? Am I . . . ?*—is to really *exit* the illusion that any of us are better than anyone, to really find and inhabit that space of, *Oh, look what consciousness is up to! Now consciousness is playing guitar and singing and singing along and dancing in the balcony and all that.*

Do you see us all, ultimately, as working to find our way back to a unified consciousness that existed before the illusions of separate beings arose?

Yeah, at this point in my life, I see existence as the same thing as relationship. Earthly existence is about the movement of energy in relationship. Identity is just a story, and it will fall away, but what endure are those relationships. We've been having them over and over and over. It is the relationships that carry from life to life, and it is *that* which is evolving.

It's not accidental that the female side of our nature—the right brain and gut-brain—and then, by default, a lot of women, and by default, feminism—is focused on relationship. This aspect allows us to be present with each other and counterbalance the stories of the left brain. The tales of the ego. The left brain is the storyteller, the one that invents our identities and, in turn, this hierarchy of identities. The whole, *I'm above animal, and animal's above plant,* and so on. That's just an idea [*laughs*]. It's just another fucking convolution of the left brain. But meanwhile, the right brain is like, *I'm here now, and you're here now, and Lefty's here now. And look at how consciousness is experiencing itself! Behold the conversation it's having.* I might be pontificating too much, but that's basically the way I think of it. And in my best moments, I can carry that out onstage and be like, *It doesn't matter if Ani DiFranco sucks, because Ani DiFranco is not real. So I don't have to worry about that anymore. Let's just have fun* [*laughs*].

It's so refreshing to hear someone like you say that you don't really exist. I mean, of course you exist in many ways and for many people, and that is deeply important. But for someone like you—who is doing so much and has done so much and will do so much—to just say, "It's an illusion," is amazing. Even in our first conversation, you went straight into it, talking about how, basically, we're all apparitions.

Yeah, well, I have to put that stuff to the side, because people don't just praise me, trust me! Sometimes it's quite the opposite. But it's like when you heard my music and responded—it's because you recognized something in my song that's also in you. Some people project onto me, or they hold me up, because I'm reflecting a part of themselves that they haven't been able to find reflected back in the culture, and they really want that part affirmed. And there it is. So I'm going to hold them up. But really, the point is, it's in *you*, and you saw it there, and that was the thrill—that you found yourself in the world around you.

Then, for other people, that's the same reason why they point fingers and why they call names, because somebody else is reflecting a part of themselves that they hate or are suppressing, or haven't come to terms with. That's a classic—it gets so surreal. The right-wing crazies are shining examples of pointing around at everyone else and describing exactly what they, themselves, are doing.

I guess the simple point is that we only see and interact with and have responses to that which we are. The responses might be positive, and they might be negative, but it's all about that dynamic of mirroring. And if you can follow that concept to its ultimate infinity, you actually are everything, and everything is you. Which is why it's so ironic when a fan doesn't allow you to change. It's like, "You were affirming this part of me, and then you shifted in my eyes somehow and that sucks, and I'm mad at you for that." It's like, "Well, yeah, but I'm not here *for you*. I'm just here! Now that you've been unlocked by a relationship with me, it's the relationship with yourself that you need to focus on."

But it's a real paradox, the fact that you can't rely on the world around you for affirmation, and the kicker is that you can't *not* rely on the world around you for affirmation and love because the world is also you. That's actually, I think, the truer thing—that self-realization doesn't happen in a vacuum, that all is self so all love is self-love. Until you experience the existence of your mother, after you're born, you don't know that you also exist. It's only in recognizing the other that you recognize yourself. And you learn to see yourself through the eyes of others. The primacy of relationship can't be denied or ignored. And when you're not getting love, in the eyes of the other, you have to do the really esoteric and complex work of realizing that you, yourself, are just another other [*laughs*]. So to speak. Consciousness is looking at itself through your eyes, too. So you must learn to love yourself and do it for yourself, to some degree, but I think it's really hard to have positive relationships with ourselves when there are no positive feedback loops happening between ourselves and other beings.

Okay, at the risk of getting too sidetracked here, remember when [Brett] Kavanaugh was having his confirmation hearings [to be a justice on the US Supreme Court], and Christine Blasey Ford was testifying against him? She spoke so powerfully, and then the whole of the female world was lying down somewhere, moaning and nauseous from watching the patriarchy double down, again. There was this moment in her testimony that was so powerful for me. There were so, so many moments, but this one moment just hit me. It was when she was describing the experience of looking in Kavanaugh's eyes and seeing herself erased. How that imprints. It actually can severely destabilize your belief in your own existence. Or your own intrinsic value.

For people who have never experienced it, I could see how that part of her testimony could just go by. I could see how the whole world of id-driven dudes could quietly say to itself, "Even if he did do that, hold her down and grind on her, what's the big frickin' deal? He was young. He didn't even really rape her. He was drunk at a party. What's the big damage? Bitches need to get over themselves." But if you've never experienced the other side of that—being invisibilized—you have no idea how that can actually shake the foundation of your existence. Watching someone look at you and literally not see you stains your brain. You actually *experience* what it is to not exist. You can experience your own disappearance in such a profound way that you can't un-experience it, and it can be very hard, or even impossible, to recover from.

It leaves you with this deep feeling of being nothing. Like you don't matter. And then, of course, because *you actually are everything and everything is you,* you feel like *nothing* matters. You're plunged into a state of nihilism. The meaning is drained out of life. So, not only can the experience of erasure permanently alter the course of a life, or a being's ability to become itself, it can have ripple effects on the whole society. The way you behave when nothing matters is a whole other thing from how you behave when life has meaning and things do matter. Even the most subtle forms of sexism, racism, heterosexism, classism—all the isms—can have powerful, blooming ripple effects. Preventing us from achieving the state of reciprocity with each other that would lift it all higher.

There are so many things going off in my mind, and one of them is about the feedback loops and the mirroring exercise, where you serve in this role where people like to have you on a pedestal because it actually makes them feel good about a part of themselves that they're aspiring to embolden or amplify. Maybe that's in the best-case scenario. Or in the worst-case scenario, or in maybe a less optimal one, they would be using you as a surrogate to be that for them, in which case, when that mirror shifts a little bit, people don't like it—for example, when you fell in love with Goat [Ani's first husband], and he's a guy, and you're wearing lipstick because you feel like doing it.

I read what you were recently recalling about the time around the release of the Little Plastic Castle *album [in 1998], where you were talking about how people were freaking out about this kind of stuff. Of course, you address some of these things on the album itself as well. I remember that album coming out and hearing you sing, "like lipstick is a sign of my declining mind," on the song "Little Plastic Castle." And I thought, even at my young age then, What?! People are saying that to her?! But then, when people act like that, I feel like it's because they feel that they can't fully do it themselves—be whatever they're saying they want you to be—and so they're trying to recruit you to be that for them, almost in their stead. It's like they're using you as a stand-in or something, to do it for them. And that's not right. That's complete objectification—the very thing that, I guess, they were suggesting that you were doing to yourself by wearing lipstick.*

Yeah, totally. It's really interesting how easily we fall into that trap of objectifying each other. Even people who experience objectification will turn around and do it to the next person, in a different format. You see that all day long. It's a real trap of the ego.

Do you feel like people got upset with you for not just being a lesbian?

Yeah, I guess so. I think we were talking the other week about postponing the processing of trauma—like, delaying a reckoning until you're ready. I did spend a few decades responding to interviewers by saying, "No, whatever, maybe somebody somewhere was upset, but so many more people were supportive and loving about my marriage! Outrage, what outrage? Backlash, what backlash?" And in some sense, that was true. But in others, I was just postponing the processing of being shamed.

And then, the twenty-fifth anniversary reissue of *Little Plastic Castle* came out [in 2023], and I had to write a statement, and I sat down to do that, and I was like, *Oh, right. That actually sucked. That really hurt. In some ways, that was a really sucky time.* It was in this way that I realized, *Okay, well, I guess I'm ready to look at it now, twenty-five years later. Look at it and really feel it.* I was asked to write something for the announcement of the rerelease, and it took a few drafts because one of my managers, Jana, was like, "Ooh, hmm. Maybe a little negative. Maybe we're giving too much time to the naysayers" [*laughs*]. But it was the beginning of really looking at it—actually letting myself feel it. The voice of the patriarchy, calling me angry or calling me whatever names—that was a badge of honor. It gets painful when your own tribe starts calling you names and ostracizing you. That's when it stings, deep in your deepest primal core. So yeah, that was probably my first dance with my own tribe turning on me.

Do you think that there's now less of that, or do you think it comes in a different way? Like, just with people in general who stand in for something that others want them to be in terms of, say, an identity? I guess I'm thinking of the whole gender-fluidity thing. There's now less expectation that people be a fixed gender—at least, supposedly there's less expectation. I don't really witness that in my day-to-day life. But do you think that there would be more room for it now?

No! [*Laughs*] Seems like there's more of it. I mean, that was pre-Internet. In order to judge, in order to give voice to your judgments of others, you had to figure out ways to amplify your judgments. You had to make a sign, or a zine, or get a job in the media. Now, it's just a click away. We're judging each other all day long in a very amplified way. I think ostracization may be peaking now. I can't imagine what it means for a very young person to put themselves out there and immediately be thrown into global judgment of the most fierce and impersonal and unstoppable kind.

At least I had those early warm-up years, where I was just being judged by the people in the room. But, you know—*Little Plastic Castle* comes out, and from all sides it was like, "Oh, look at her, she's a fuckin' hypocrite, sellout. I knew it. I knew she was full of shit." But that era almost looks tame now, compared to the negative potential of social media. I just think, Goddess bless any young person trying to be free and express themselves in the age of outrage.

You don't really look at stuff, right? You don't read reviews of yourself, and you don't read people's comments on social media, things like that?

Almost never. People say just about everything there is to say, when you're a public person, and I'm just barely beginning to be able to look at it more matter-of-factly. To depersonalize the most negative stuff and just say, "Yup, that's what happens." But there's no way I'm going to jump into the fray. I think, once you step into that arena, you get trapped in there, just waving off one charging bull after another. I couldn't just show up and say something and then disappear and not engage with the responses and all the dialogue. And there's no doubt, it would be unkind and mean and would ultimately debilitate and crush me. I try to, sort of, put out the bare minimum I have to, to have a career in music in the twenty-first century. And I do almost all of it vicariously, through a middleman. If I could opt out of the incessant online conversation altogether, I would.

I was just wondering, too, whether your teenager uses social media, or if you encourage her to stay off it.

It's been a lot, parenting in this moment. There's a lot of trying to get their head out of the phone and back into where they're standing. But you can't, really. It's an epidemic. And I feel like my teenager is among those young people who are dissuaded from trying anything or taking risks because the stakes just seem too high.

The gotcha gun is pointed at everyone now, and it's like you can't unsay things once they're out there. Especially for a celebrity, people might just start screenshotting any particular thing you say. And then it's news, "Ani DiFranco said this," and then it takes a life of its own.

Right. You can put yourself out there, as long as you can be perfect in everything you say and do, according to everyone, everywhere, forever. Have fun, kids [*laughs*].

In your memoir, you talked about Prince being a two-spirit. I think of forces like David Bowie here, too. Did you ever relate to yourself as a two-spirit, or a multispirit, or a one-spirit with all these different aspects? Or has it always been just that you did your thing, and you didn't really have a meta-level reckoning of it in that kind of way?

I guess, on that really natural level, we are all two-spirit. That's exactly how we're designed. If you were to open up the top of your skull right now, you'd see two very separate centers of personality and perception and emotion and reaction and understanding. There are two of you in there. Or, like we talked about before, you could conceive of the head-brain and the gut-brain. Anyway, we have two very distinct internal-processing hardware systems, with very distinct natures. This bifurcated intelligence, I believe, is the genius of our species, and it is, first and foremost, the genius of the two-spirit. Some humans embody it more vividly than others—and dare I say, these beings often have access to more elevated states of consciousness, becoming our most celebrated artists, re: Prince and David Bowie.

    The trouble with brain science, and all sciences, is that they were overwhelmingly devised by men alone, men who are not feminists. Men who have not yet glimpsed some gaping holes in their inquiry. They are not given to notice the relationship between gender and patriarchy and even the hardest of their hard sciences. I mean, that's why I keep trying to talk to people about patriarchy as being the first wrong turn, from which all other wrong turns in our thinking may follow. Like, you can't get to peace on earth from here—because way, way back, we muzzled one half of our nature. We have to achieve a balance between the energies, within and amongst us, before we can go and fix the rest. Yet we keep trying to address—fill in the blank—climate change, economic exploitation, racism—and achieve a state of balance, from a global state of imbalance.

This is why I called a chapter in my book "The Alphabet vs. the Goddess," after the book by Leonard Shlain. He is a remarkable exception to this history of looking at the world with a patch over one eye. He is a scientist and a feminist, and he starts by confronting the written word—the basic building block of scientific knowledge—as a masculine tool with a masculine predisposition. As in: language itself stems from the masculine part of our nature, so beware where it takes you. Don't turn off your gut! With the advent of the written word, we have become so lost in the stories of our left hemispheres, we've become further and further detached from the living world. Isolated in worlds of our own abstraction. Logic is powerful, but it's also the way we got to this place of crises. Everything out of balance. The knowing presence—which operates wordlessly—the voice of intuition, has long been drowned out. If you think about it, though, it's no wonder that, since the right brain doesn't have words to describe what it knows, it can never win the argument [*laughs*].

But it can move through things like music and the spiritual arts and energies and phenomena like that, right? And take up residence and break through the frozen storehouses of language?

Yes, exactly. And it can know exponentially more than the story it was born into. It can use the left brain's logic, but also all kinds of other awareness or intuition or shit that we can't even fucking explain. About telepathy, about spooky action at a distance, about knowing that something just happened to your loved one on the other side of the country, or what's going to happen in the future.

Isn't it so beautiful that it can't be subdued in that way, that it breaks through?

Well, right. Hopefully, it breaks through. But I think of the degree to which it has been subdued—even within women, for instance. I think there's a longstanding history of just sort of the general gaslighting of the female experience within patriarchy, and we can absolutely unlearn our connection with our gut. We can absolutely let that voice be muffled to the point of inaudible. That profound sense of numbing or disconnect is a huge part of the story of being female within patriarchy.

Chapter 6

Spiritual Intentions and Manifesting Reality in Art and Life

In this last conversation, Ani and I turned to more of her recent work, which often overtly addresses spiritual topics. We juxtaposed these explorations with discussions of songs from her earliest albums, in which she feels that she was often writing into being a version of herself. To write it and sing it and truly feel it is to become it.

She shared how, in her early work, she wrote to conjure a force field around her, to feel safe as she navigated the world. Many of her earlier songs blend an intense and moving vulnerability with an unflinching back-up-don't-mess-with-me vibe. She reflected on how all of this was by design, if subconscious, as she was determined to be an autonomous, fearless, intrepid person who would chart her own way forward. And that, she did and continues to do.

Ani spoke of how she projects intentions from her spirit into the world around her, which helps her to cocreate realities that she desires. She also sets intentions for her art, channeling the spiritual vitalities and their purposes into songs, poems, and performances.

The conversation included Ani's impassioned and frank thoughts on reproductive freedom and ended with a return to her understanding of all that exists as relational. A unified field of consciousness separates, only temporarily, to experience itself in other discrete manifestations. And for this process to be peaceful and productive, energies must be able to dynamically circulate. When energies are blocked, destruction and violence ensue. The creative energy of relationality, when flowing in reciprocity, is the most authentically liberating force in art and life.

I would love to talk with you today about the most recent era of your albums, such as Binary *(2017) and* Revolutionary Love *(2021). It's great how these albums include songs about things like consciousness, telepathy, and the powers that are within us and run through us. Is there a time at which you would say you started thinking about things in a more expressly spiritual way, even though you always experienced these types of things—for example, when you started calling these things spiritual in your mind? Or is it hard to say?*

I guess I just don't even know half the time what to label things. But I do agree that my spiritual self or whatever has been evolving as long as I've been on the planet. But no, I never worried about what to label it, or when something was beginning or ending—or I don't know [*laughs*]. I just have new thoughts and new awarenesses. It's like the longer you're here, and the more experiences you have, and the more experiences of others you witness, the deeper your intuitive understanding of things.

I was just thinking of some lines from back in the day in the nineties, in your song "Willing to Fight" [on the 1993 album Puddle Dive*]:*

> the windows of my soul
> are made of one way glass
> don't bother looking into my eyes
> if there's something you wanna know, just ask

I thought that was so powerful. I was wondering if it was a conscious shield you put up, or if you just knew that you were impenetrable by other people in that way.

Well, first of all, that is a crock of bull [*laughs*]. I think it's like wishful songwriting. I am absolutely, totally, and utterly accessible—through my eyes, my ears, my elbows [*laughs*]. But that was when I was young, and I was trying to write myself into safety. There are so many songs from back in the day that are about developing—or at least projecting—a force field. There are so many examples. "If He Tries Anything" is one. It's a message of reassurance to another woman, like, "I will protect you cuz I've *got* this." But the truth of my young self was actually very different from that. I was still totally vulnerable and open and smiley! That's why I needed to sing myself messages of being strong and tough, even invincible—not just to mind-meld other people, but to mind-meld myself.

It's funny. I revived that song "Willing to Fight" recently because of the twenty-fifth anniversary of *Living in Clip*. I was bringing it back out onstage, but singing those lines is like—I was sort of messing with them, reworking them for the now, to see if I could find a new approach that made them ring true in my ears. "*don't bother looking into my eyes*," I mean, I know why I wrote those lines—I was fashioning a force field of self-protection. But more recently, I was trying to sing them in a way that felt more like, *Don't assume that you understand me because, quite likely, you don't.*

I feel like people project a lot of things onto me, whether they are the projections of the dominant culture and patriarchy, or the projections of a feminist or queer subculture or whatever. So I guess there's something in there, in that song, that still resonates with me. The place where those lines still hold true is in that feeling of, *Don't assume you know.*

Or try to invade you.

Yeah. But the whole idea of having a tough skin or being impenetrable is simply a wish of mine [*laughs*]. That's never really been true.

Do you ever summon—or do you ask for or set an intention for—a protective field around you? Or is it kind of automatic because of all these years of projecting this intention around yourself?

I think I do set intentions in various ways. I've been aware for a long time that intentions are a big part of the game, so sometimes it's literally that I'm walking down a dark street alone, and I'm just trying to project that I'm okay and that I'm safe and that I'm in control of the situation and myself. I project a force field of solid self-possession and positivity to the menacing forces of the world—*Not this one. Not now.*

It comes in many forms. Sometimes, before I go onstage and I feel nervous and I feel self-doubt, and I worry about coming across that way—maybe it's a weird situation that I'm performing in, to new people or whatever. Or maybe I'm just feeling insecure that they won't be into it. But then I'll try to get myself to the place of, *You're a good person with good intentions, and you're just going to try to do some music. Just go out there with a pure heart and just trust that that will communicate itself, somehow.* That's the kind of intention vibe that I'll try to set, walking onstage.

You talk about how you have many different voices, and how your voice changes throughout the day, even hour by hour. Do you think of those as different streams of consciousness coming through, almost like different beings or channels of energy?

I guess I would say that it's just different patterns of thought that are affecting my experience. I think that if I was not prey to overthinking things, maybe I would have a more stable baseline. I would be calmer and more in touch, on a reliable basis, with a sort of unconditional love for myself and for the world. But I think that I'm at the mercy of a lot of thoughts about myself, about the world, about life, its struggles, and they can spin negative. I have a lot of self-doubts that I think get in the way of singing and being all the way present.

Do you sometimes feel like the songs sing you—as though, as they're coming forth, they're still congealing or coming together and then, at some point, they're in full fruition? And is it like this at times, whether you're in a semi-trance or fully awake?

Yeah, both happen. It's a reciprocal relationship, for sure. The songs used me to write them, and they sing me, like you asked. And then, also, the opposite is happening.

I found that to be true of my literal *human* creations, too [*laughs*]. Because I also made a couple of babies along the way—and my experience of pregnancy, in the beginning—it's sort of like your body is doing something. Your body is just doing this radical thing. But then, at some point, it becomes more relational. For some time, it's like you're making something, but you're also slowly, more and more, being possessed by something! You're both creating and being created. Which is exactly true, I think, since pregnancy and childbirth are the actual *lived* experiences of oneness. Part of you is the part creating, and part of you is the part being created.

This new wave of fascists in America, taking away women's reproductive freedom, they predicate their case on the notion of a fetus as an autonomous individual, whose interests can run contrary to those of its mother, but that's the height of egoic, patriarchal stupidity to me. The fetus *is* the mother, and the mother *is* the fetus! Their interests are one and the same! It's just so depressing. Not just on the level of all the needless trauma to women, but also, how are we ever gonna recognize the inherent oneness of all forms of consciousness if we can't even recognize the oneness of a pregnant mother and child?

I have this new song called "Baby Roe" that I wrote after reading this epic book called *The Family Roe*, by Joshua Prager. *The Family Roe* is a really well-researched and well-written book about the backstory behind the Supreme Court's *Roe v. Wade* decision of 1972. It follows all the relevant characters through the unfolding story of events, and it's just fascinating. One of the many people we get to know in the book is Norma McCorvey's ("Jane Roe's") baby. This was the baby she was actually forced to have and then give up for adoption—because the process of winning the right to have an abortion took longer than her pregnancy. She had to have a baby while fighting for the right not to. Anyway, this baby was adopted and didn't find out, until she was an adult, about the role she played in history. As you can imagine, the antichoice contingent was keen to get their hands on her—thinking she would be the ultimate spokesperson for their cause. But she wasn't. Even knowing that she would have been aborted, had her birth mother been free to do so, Baby Roe remains prochoice. And I know, if I was her, I would be, too. There's this part in the song that goes:

> *and if you think this life*
> *is your only life*
> *you're a fool*
> *spirit can't be stopped*
> *no matter who gives birth*
> *to who*
> *no, spirit won't be stopped*
> *no matter who gives birth*
> *to who*

And I just really believe that. Spirit is not reliant on any specific form, or any potentially specific form, to manifest. It is manifesting all the time to its fullest. The path of compassion becomes about mitigating suffering and trauma. People who promote the idea that forcing women to bear unwanted children is somehow a reduction of harm, instead of an escalation, are just people who have one, or both, eyes covered. It's the very logic and culture of the people whose eyes erase you when they look at you. Anyway, I do feel songs and human babies are related in some way. Both can inform us about the nature of creation, the process of making room for spirit to come through.

And with art, as with human children, there's often a gestation period. Like, whether it's a poem or painting or song or album. So you'll maybe start getting seeds of the spirit coming through, or there's fertilization that happens and something's growing and you're aware of it, but it has yet to be given full embodiment in the world, as an external existence.

Yeah. In terms of the gestation period of writing, there's a meditation that starts running in the background, and then you start looking for it in the world—and then you start wondering how to describe this thing that you feel. Then, at some point, there's sort of an event, where you enter the creative space, and you elect to interact with it, and you try to bring in that energy. I don't mean to make it sound too dramatic or spooky. I'm just trying to describe something very subtle. Anyway, my experience of songwriting is that there is, if you're lucky, a concise moment where the gestating becomes birthing. You just sit down and do it.

I found writing a book to be very different from writing songs. It was just a way different pace and level of patience. There was so much just sitting there and tapping on the keyboard and staring off into space. It was harder to discern a moment where something was happening, or tell any moment from any other. I would just keep circling around and around and around and around, closer and closer and closer, refining and refining this big sprawling thing. I mean, there would be flashes of, *Oh, wait, I know how I have to do this, or how I get there.* There would be little inspirational moments of, *Oh, wait, I know what I have to do here,* but the pace was just so much more prolonged. I had to become a whole new species of writer, with a different gestational period [*laughs*].

Do you ever have experiences when you're writing, though, where you also feel like you're just downloading? When it comes onto the page, and then you say, Oh, okay, great. I didn't know I was thinking that concept, or in that way.

No, I wish I could just actually go like, *Whoa, holy cow! What was that? That came through in like a ten-page chunk!* But no, not really. For me, it was more like, *H. I. Yes, "hi." Let me think, hi. Is that hi? Yeah, hi. "Hi there." Okay!* [*Laughs*]

It's excruciating. I don't have nearly the experience with that type of gestation and birth—the complete-sentences racket—that I do with poems and songs. So no, I don't really have moments where my fingers are flying across the keyboard and pages are spitting out. When I have to write something—and I do all kinds of frickin' writing. Right now, I'm involved in an effort with my kids' school, to save it from horrible leadership [*laughs*]. It really is like this sort of Trumpian man has taken over this poor school. And he's muzzling teachers, and he's squashing student protests; I'm writing essays and letters to the administration. And it takes me all night to make three frickin' paragraphs! So that's my experience. I'm hoping that maybe, at some point, I can open up the aperture and let it flow more easily in the realm of sentences and paragraphs.

For me, I feel like I eventually passed a threshold where the prose writing could flow more easily, probably from having to engage in it so much over the years [laughs]. One of my guides once explained to me that I was transferring wisdom to a dense form, imprinting it in words on a page. At first, I took offense—Dense?! [laughs]—but then she explained what she meant: the writing was akin to converting light into words that convey meaning through physical materials in this dense gravitational space called earth. I don't know if you ever passed through a sort of similar threshold with your music. It sounds like you were just flowing with it from a very young age.

I think that word, "dense," is very telling. I feel like words have a density, and you're trying to take things, often, that are ethereal, that are hard to hold onto. They're things you sense and things you feel in a space beyond words, and you're trying to solidify them and lock them into place on the page. So there's sort of a density and a weight to it, which can be somewhat artificial or even counterproductive. But that's what we have to do to share our ideas with each other in that way. We have words, and they're like these coarse blocks, and you're trying to explain water with them.

It's like what you convey in your lyrics in "Hour Follows Hour"—"you wouldn't try to put the ocean in a paper cup"—though I know the topic was different in that song [on the 1995 album Not a Pretty Girl*]. I also was wondering: would you use this phrase of spirit guides for yourself, or does that not really apply to your perspective or experience?*

I guess it doesn't really apply because I don't think I have—I mean, I hope to, before my deathbed. To have more of a one-on-one with my spirit guides and actually be able to interact with them. But I don't. It's not that tangible to me.

So there's something maybe loose that you feel informs your knowing and gut-brain?

Yeah, it just feels like instinct. It feels like intuition. It feels like, yeah, my gut. And I think, on the other side of the coin, I've realized that, when I feel conflicted, which I have a lot in my life—about things, relationships—that's me trying to disobey my gut [*laughs*]. It's me trying to tune out the information which is coming in. My brain is thinking that I have to do something, and the whole rest of my being is vibrating, *No!* [*Laughs*] And then, my brain will talk to itself out in the world, about how conflicted it is and how hard it is to make a decision. But it's not really hard. It's only hard when you are in perpetual denial. I can be locked in that state for a long time, actually. But at least now, I can diagnose it more quickly. It's like you're fighting your own wisdom.

Aside from your father, do you ever communicate with or feel the presence of other ancestors? I was just looking back at "Willing to Fight," where you sing:

> i got strangers for great-grandchildren
> i got strangers for ancestors

Is there anything you'd like to share about what you meant with those lines?

Yeah, I never knew my grandparents on this plane. They all died early, or I was born late or something. I missed that party. So I have senses of them. I have some vague senses of who they were, through my parents. But no, I don't feel like I've met them or their spirits in a tangible way. I can only guess about them.

I wrote that line when I was very young, but as it happens, I had kids late, too, so if they have kids someday, I may not know them for long or at all. I certainly won't know *their* kids. So, I do feel a little marooned in time. I think I was right about that.

When you were young, did you have a sense of an afterlife, or that there would be a spirit realm that you would cross into at the end?

I feel like I've always understood that death is not an end and that, just like everything in the whole freakin' universe, it came from somewhere, and it goes to somewhere, and it pretty much does that infinitely [laughs].

It's hard to put myself back to being a kid, but I think I was way more skeptical when I was young, about all the things that were not a part of my limited culture—like talking to spirit and hearing their response, or reincarnation—things that were not a part of the dominant culture that I grew up in. I probably thought that these things were malarkey until I got a little older and realized that the story is way more complex and mysterious than a lot of science and Western religion allow for.

I was just looking at the lyrics to "If He Tries Anything" [from the 1994 album Out of Range*] and wondering if these lines were purely metaphorical, or if you didn't really overthink them, if they just came through. There's a line where you sing, "the goddesses will come up to the ripped screen door," in the sequence:*

> tell you one thing
> i'm gonna make noise when i go down
> for ten square blocks
> they're gonna know i died
> all the goddesses will come up
> to the ripped screen door
> and say, what do you want dear?
> and i'll say, i want inside

What's wild is that, again, you're picking—I mean, that's another bit that, in a literal sense, is totally untrue. Something that I know about myself is that the behavior of freezing—the physiological danger responses were defined as "fight or flight" for a long time, right? Coming from a masculine perspective. And those are two biggies for sure, but more recently "freeze and fawn" were added to the list. And I think that freezing is actually my predominant response. I have had experiences where—there was one time when I was sort of on my way to drowning. I was in the ocean, and I'm not a strong swimmer at all. I was trying to swim out to this raft because the two people I was with were doing that. Oh, it was actually Goat and Compton—on Bequia! And I got halfway out, and the waves were pretty big, and I just started swallowing water. And I just started panicking. But I was too embarrassed to cry for help. I thought, *Oh, wow, dude. Is this the part where you literally die of embarrassment? That is too pathetic!* So I made myself yell, but it was hard. Anyway, I can picture myself in a state of quiet surrender. It's harder to picture myself screaming and fighting—defending myself. I don't know why.

So I think, there again, you pointed out a lyric in a song where I'm trying to write myself into a different state of being. I'm trying to write myself into power. But when I'm stranded at an airport and it's a blizzard, and there are crowds of people who can't all make it out of there, and all the hotels are filled because everybody else is in the same predicament, and there are only a few seats left—some people push to the front, and I'm just not that guy. I might be standing in the front and still let people push past me.

But there is a strong, self-possessed version of you, right? I was just looking at the same album, Out of Range, *with the song by the same title, and you sing:*

> i was locked
> into being my mother's daughter
> i was just eating bread and water
> thinking nothing ever changes
> and i was shocked
> to see the mistakes of each generation

will just fade like a radio station
when you drive out of range

That's another big empowerment song, I think, for a lot of us. Certainly, for me, this idea that bullshit can just fade like a radio station when we drive away from it—whatever the bullshit is. It doesn't matter who is the source of the bullshit, or allegedly the source of the bullshit, but it all just fades like a station going out of signal.

Yeah, right. And yes, it actually totally works. You *can* create yourself. Or recreate yourself. So yes, the person who wrote the line about the eyes, or the lines *"for ten square blocks they're gonna know i died . . ."*—that person wrote me into being. And yeah, I think I am pretty much that person now [*laughs*].

But seriously, I think it's a process to exit your conditioning and shed the constraints of fear or passivity or whatever—all the toxic socialization and hierarchies and assumptions. I've seen my songs help people through that process, in the same way that they have helped me. That's what I meant before, about my focus being on healing myself, from the beginning. It was about getting something out of me that was hurting me or not serving me. It wasn't about putting on a show for someone else. It was about healing. And I think all those songs, singing them over and over and over, kind of worked.

So, it was like medicine for yourself to come more fully into yourself than you already had. And then also, you were sending this medicine in songs out to other people to activate and empower them. That's beautiful. And these radio stations of our pasts that are fading, they could be broadcasting content from anyone. It could be teachers in your daughter's school system, whoever is involved in trying to muzzle the students in the ways that you're mentioning. It's really inspiring to hear that you're fighting against that right now. I think it's one of the most toxic things, trying to muzzle people at a young age and attempting to convince them that it's fine that they're muzzled.

Yes, exactly. The students spontaneously organized a rally and a demonstration, no help from adults. They walked out. To protest some horrible things that the school leadership did. And then, the school leadership gave them all detention and threatened to suspend them all for skipping class while they were holding this walkout. And my daughter and about two other kids boycotted the detention. She got suspended, but I fully supported her in that.

That's amazing that she did that.

Yeah, they want to control the narrative, and they want to control people's actions. And yeah, my daughter, I'm very glad that she's invested in the process of saying, "No, you don't control everything." It's painful, this time we're living in. There's a global tussle, trying to wrest power out of the hands of a very small minority.

A small minority trying so hard to control things but becoming obsolete and outdated, thankfully, in the face of all the changes that are happening. I'm so grateful to your daughter and to all those who, like her, are doing the work.

Yeah, I am, too [laughs]. I think of all sorts of young women who are just like, "No, I'm doing this my way, and by my own measure. Your authority and your value system don't apply to me." They're challenging the patriarchy in so many ways. There are people everywhere pushing their way in. So, it's like: *It's on.* This new generation is unleashing the true power of diversity—in so many ways—and all the forms of oppression and backward thinking are being upheaved. There's a radical shift happening. Ironically, I think it's largely driven by these gizmos that we all carry around in our pockets, that are also killing us [laughs]. They are also making us crazy and sucking our brains out! But, because we have the whole world in our pocket now, at least the whole world can no longer be denied.

I was wondering, too, with your daughter or others close to you, whether you regularly experience heart-to-heart communication that occurs beyond spoken language. In "Binary," you sing about conversing with the heart. Is this something that you feel on a semi-regular basis with other beings—something like a heart connection and a conversation that goes beyond the language of the tongue?

Oh, definitely. I mean, that's at least half of what's happening in a face-to-face conversation—energy exchange. The words are icing. For me, because I'm so focused on the energy level, sometimes I have to almost exit the conversation before I can hear all the words. My perception, in the moment, is really focused on energy.

But I also do have a kind of—people talk about a photographic memory. I have the audio version. Afterward, I can hear the whole thing over again, and then, of course, I can't help but think of what a better use of words would've been, on my part. That's one of my fucking pathologies—the three-blocks-later syndrome! Because I have that element of sort of freezing, when my adrenaline goes up, if I'm just talking to somebody—that brings me up a notch. So, whatever, my whole life I've felt like I've never known what to say in the moment. I just sort of speak without thinking clearly and then, when I leave the conversation, it all becomes clear, exactly what was said and what I wish I'd said instead [*laughs*]. I don't know if you can relate at all.

Very much. I have something similar with the replays, almost like streaming them. With this conversing from the heart that you're talking about, I was also thinking of the idea of completing the circuit, which you also sing about in "Binary":

> you gotta complete the circuit
> not just with human beings
> with the sky above you
> with the earth beneath your feet
> when you complete the circuit
> with everything that lives
> borders get blurry
> and the rest is adjectives

Were you thinking about tapping in, even to the heart or the soul of the sky and the earth? What does completing the circuit mean for you?

Well, first, let me pause for a second and just say thanks for even asking about my recent records. It's hard to be an artist and a songwriter and an album-maker for thirty years and have people continue to track what you do. I just think it's a hard thing. I've been around for a long time, and I've released more than twenty records. So I hear a lot from people, like, "Oh, you got me through high school," or, "Once upon a time, you meant everything to me." I feel I do better and better work as I go, in some ways, and the things that mean the most to me are all in the present. But people talk about the past a lot, and my past work—when I was busting a hole in a paradigm.

And yeah, that song "Binary"—I just really feel like an uninhibited, well-balanced flow is what peace is. That's the meaning of the word. And the whole process of flow, at its highest frequency, centers around love and compassion. That sort of unconditional love that we come from and return to—when it's not able to cycle between things—between you and yourself, between you and the one in front of you, between you and the greater world, between the world and itself—therein lies the damage. Love has to flow and keep flowing, or else it's like the most powerful energy pent up, with nowhere to go, ready to explode, causing violence and destruction.

But the good news is, when loving energy is flowing uninhibited and cycling freely between things, there is an exponential leap of possibility. As Robin Wall Kimmerer so brilliantly illuminates in *Braiding Sweetgrass*, reciprocity is the key. It's the state that transforms everything. A state of reciprocity can make most solutions just appear. Ask any married couple. It makes navigating anything possible.

I saw this documentary recently, called *The Biggest Little Farm*, and it was so inspiring. Just following the story of this couple trying to remake their lives in the modern world into a steady flow of reciprocity with all of consciousness. Trying to participate in nature and cooperate toward mutual abundance. It really shows how incredibly transformative a state of reciprocity can be. You see the life-giving transformation of the land before your eyes.

Can I tell you one more little story? There was this organization, a women's organization, that recently offered me a little money to help spread awareness about something. Some event or legislation or something. I can't even remember. And that sounds weird just even coming out of my mouth right now, but it was an acknowledgment of the work it takes to be an activist. It wasn't a lot of money. It was a little honorarium—a symbol—but it had a noticeable impact on my mental state. I immediately thought, *How cool of them to offer that! I will accept the honorarium and donate it back to the organization.*

So, okay, whatever, I did the PSA. The same kind of thing that I do all day long, but the revelation for me was how different it felt in my body. Held within the structure of reciprocity, it felt lighter. The task felt easier, the gift more freely given, instead of like one last bit of energy the world was trying to extract from me. I don't mean to make it sound like being an activist is a drag. I'm just saying that there can be an element, after so many years of fighting for things, of just feeling drained. Of being asked to always give more and more. There can be this constriction within me, this defensive tightening in my chest. This can make you feel like all your energy is being taken from you. I'm not sure if that's the best example, or if I'm explaining myself well, but I do believe that a reciprocal state of respect and compassion is transformative. Reciprocity—the state of mutual gift-giving—is joyful and expansive.

Afterword

Visions for Our Times

The entire arc of our collaboration for this book was an exercise in generative reciprocity of the most delightful kind. Our dialogues unfolded around unified themes, and they did so almost entirely organically. The conversations, as with the conception and fruition of the whole project, felt thoroughly spirit-led and spir*ited*, as I hope they feel to you. For me, these forms of creative vitality are synonymous with life itself. The cycles of giving birth to this book with Ani were no exception.

Throughout this book, Ani has lifted the veils on many of the mysteries and treasures of her creative processes, opening to our view the ethereal and sublime dimensions of her life that many artists keep covered or otherwise hidden from view. Her generosity and authenticity in opening dimensions of her spiritual experiences and intuitive gifts mirror her broader openness and vulnerability as a profoundly human and visionary artist for our times. Rarely is someone who is as badass and celebrated as Ani also so open and relatable, so available to the world, and so forthright in her own searching. She does not claim to have all the answers to the enigmas of the universe and its spiritual dimensions. Instead, she invites us into the distinctive experiential universe of her prism as spirit, artist, human.

Toward the close of our book-writing journey, Ani shared the November 2023 edition of her new-moon letter with a group of her subscribers on Patreon. She writes a letter to her patrons every new moon and shares with them two as-yet-unheard recordings. These may be some of her new songs, or unreleased songs, or unreleased versions of known songs. That month, the offerings were "Please Say Yes," by her mentor Michael Meldrum, and a version of her song "Reckoning." What she imparted in the accompanying letter, to my mind, resonated with several of the themes that course throughout these conversations, charged like adjoining electrical currents or circuits—interconnectivity, oneness, multivocality, intuitive communication, freedom, and the spiritual wisdom of nature. Reflecting upon her two recordings, Ani wrote of the many voices that are detectable in her art and life over the years:

> *As I listen to them, it strikes me how different the singing is on the two . . . and how many voices each of us uses over the course of our lives. (Or how many voices use us?) The voice is so infinitely changeable and expressive an instrument! And how epic is it that our species seems to be influencing other species to use their voices more and in more varied ways. Not just dogs and cats! . . . And how cool that much of what we learned about the possibilities of vocalizing, we learned from birds! What goes around, comes around. Ah, to live in open dialogue with all of consciousness! To really return to a state where all species are in the flow with each other. Where humans are actively listening and paying attention, not just talking over the rest. Phew. Imagine the possibilities . . . When I run for president, my platform will be to increase interspecies dialogue, understanding, equity, and peace. Start there.*

These evocative words appeared in Ani's handwriting, inscribed in brown marker on torn-out sheets of a spiral notebook. For me, the letter's form and content are emblematic of the multifaceted dimensions of the spirit of Ani—flowing and ever-expanding, open to the interconnectedness of all and seemingly limitless in her visions of potential worlds and ways of living.

Acknowledgments

We are grateful to the wonderful array of people who helped to bring this book into the world. We give so many thanks to Peter Casperson, Ani's visionary manager and a key guide for this project, and to Peter's team at Invasion Group. We also give thanks to our sage literary agents, Jennifer Gates and Sarah Lazin, as well as their team at Aevitas Creative Management. Gratitude is also due to Ani's amazing team at Righteous Babe Records and to our publisher, Akashic Books, including the inspired Johnny Temple, Aaron Petrovich, and their team. Many thanks also to Susan Alzner, Dana Flor, and Andrew Macpherson for permission to use their beautiful photographs in the book. Lauren gives gratitude to her family, friends, and interlocutors, as well as her beloved husband, Jeffrey Rosen.

Discography

Albums (all released on Righteous Babe Records)

Ani DiFranco, 1990
Not So Soft, 1991
Imperfectly, 1992
Puddle Dive, 1993
Like I Said, 1993
Out of Range, 1994
Not a Pretty Girl, 1995
Dilate, 1996
More Joy, Less Shame, 1996
Living in Clip, 1997
Little Plastic Castle, 1998
Up Up Up Up Up Up, 1999
Little Plastic Castle Remixes, 1999
To the Teeth, 1999
Swing Set EP, 2000
Revelling/Reckoning, 2001
So Much Shouting, So Much Laughter, 2002
Evolve, 2003
Educated Guess, 2004
Knuckle Down, 2005
Reprieve, 2006
Canon, 2007
Red Letter Year, 2008
¿Which Side Are You On?, 2012
Allergic to Water, 2014
Binary, 2017
No Walls Mixtape, 2019
Revolutionary Love, 2021
Ani DiFranco (thirtieth anniversary edition), 2021
Living in Clip (twenty-fifth anniversary edition), 2022
Little Plastic Castle (twenty-fifth anniversary edition), 2023
Unprecedented Sh!t, 2024

Official Bootlegs

Atlanta, GA, 10.09.03, 2004
Sacramento, CA, 10.25.03, 2004
Portland, OR, 4.7.04, 2004
Boston, MA, 11.16.03, 2005
Chicago, IL, 1.17.04, 2005
Madison, WI, 1.25.04, 2005
Rome, Italy, 11.15.04, 2005
Carnegie Hall, New York, NY, 4.6.02, 2006
Boston, MA, 11.10.06, 2007
Hamburg, Germany, 10.18.07, 2008
Saratoga, NY, 9.16.06, 2009
Chicago, IL, 9.22.07, 2009
Buffalo, NY, 4.22.12, 2013
London, England, 10.29.08, 2013
Ridgefield, CT, 11.18.09, 2014
Harrisburg, PA, 1.23.08, 2014
New York, NY, 3.30.95, 2015
Glenside, PA, 11.11.12, 2016
Melbourne, FL, 1.19.16, 2016
Bootleg Live in Charlottesville, 5.12.18, 2018
Bootleg Live in Woodstock, 6.16.19, 2019
Bootleg Live in Keene, 11.16.19, 2020
Revolutionary Love: Live at Big Blue, 1.27.21–1.28.21, 2021

Videos

Render, 2002
Trust: Live in Washington, DC, 2004
Live at Babeville, 2008
Revolutionary Love: Live at Big Blue, 2021

Books by Ani DiFranco

Verses (Seven Stories, 2007)
No Walls and the Recurring Dream: A Memoir (Penguin, 2019)
The Knowing (Penguin, 2023)
Show Up and Vote (Penguin, 2024)

Book, Film, and Art References

The Biggest Little Farm, documentary directed by John Chester and written by Mark Monroe and John Chester (LD Entertainment/FarmLore Films/Impact Partners/Artemis Rising Foundation, 2019).

Coyne, Petah. *Above and Beneath the Skin* exhibition. Further information on the January 16–April 10, 2005, exhibition at SculptureCenter in Long Island City, NY, available at: https://www.sculpture-center.org/exhibitions/3058/above-and-beneath-the-skin. (Last accessed February 4, 2025).

DiFranco, Ani. *No Walls and the Recurring Dream: A Memoir* (Penguin, 2019).

DiFranco, Ani. *The Knowing* (Penguin, 2023).

Kimmerer, Robin Wall. *Braiding Sweetgrass: Indigenous Wisdom, Scientific Knowledge, and the Teachings of Plants* (Milkweed Editions, 2013).

Lacan, Jacques. *The Seminar of Jacques Lacan: The Ethics of Psychoanalysis (Book VII)*, edited by Jacques-Alain Miller and translated by Dennis Porter (W.W. Norton & Company, 1997).

Love, Lizzo, documentary featuring Lizzo and directed by Doug Pray (Live Nation Productions/Boardwalk Pictures/Warner Music Entertainment/Atlantic Films/Diamond Docs, 2022).

Prager, Joshua. *The Family Roe: An American Story* (W.W. Norton & Company, 2021).

Prince. *The Beautiful Ones*, edited by Dan Piepenbring (One World/Penguin Random House, 2019).

Shlain, Leonard. *The Alphabet Versus the Goddess: The Conflict Between Word and Image* (Penguin, 1999).

Van Zandt, Townes. "Pancho and Lefty," on the album *The Late Great Townes Van Zandt* (Poppy Records, 1972).

Coda
Lyrics for Songs Referenced

baby roe

i think we might be wrong about all of it
in fact, it's been proven
keeps coming down to this shitty little interface
that we're usin
the very edges of our knowing
is just the tiny tip that's showing
but we're so wigged out
yeah, we're so devout
to this waking dream
what's playing on the screen

and you just never know
do you, baby roe?
it's all absurd
but even you maintain
timing is everything
when you're steppin
off a curb
and if you think this life
is your only life
you're a fool
no, spirit can't be stopped
no matter who gives birth to who
no, spirit won't be stopped
no matter who gives birth to who

the path of least suffering
leaves the best trail
the path of least suffering
it don't matter which side of the veil
it don't matter which side of the veil

i think we might be wrong about all of it

telepathic

i'll just be going along
lookin through my eyes
through my eyes
then i'll go inside of someone
and i'll look through their eyes
through their eyes
they might be behind a counter
they might be filled with disdain
goin behind the eyes of people
is a dangerous game
it's a dangerous game
goin behind the eyes of people
is a dangerous game

we live in a world full of longing
we live in a world full of fear
so many sheep in wolves' clothing
hiding behind a wolf's sneer
i wish i was not telepathic
i wish i was lost in a dream
i gotta stop paying attention
just keep takin hits for the team
i'll just be going along
lookin through my eyes
through my eyes
then i'll go inside of someone
and i'll look through their eyes
through their eyes
they might be behind a counter
they might be filled with disdain
goin behind the eyes of people
is a dangerous game
it's a dangerous game
goin behind the eyes of people
is a dangerous game

everest

from the depth of the pacific
to the height of everest
still the world is smoother
than a shiny ball bearing
so i take a few steps back
put on a wider lens
and it changes your skin
your sex and what you're wearing
and distance shows your silhouette
to be a lot like mine
like a sphere is a sphere
and all of us here
have been here all the time
yeah, we've been here all the time

you brought me to church
cinder blocks, fluorescent light
you brought me to church
at seven o'clock on sunday night
and the band was rockin
and the floors were scrubbed clean
and everybody had a tambourine

so i took a deep breath
and became the white girl with the hair
and you sat right beside me
while everybody stared
and through the open window
i think the singing went outside
and floated up to tell
all the stars not to hide
cuz by the time church let out
the sky was much clearer

and the moon was so beautiful
the ocean held up a mirror
and as we walked home
we spoke slowly
we spoke slow
and we spoke lowly
like it was taking more time
than usual to choose
words to go
with your squeaky sandal shoes
like time is not a thing
that's ours to lose

from the height of the pacific
to the depths of everest

32 flavors

squint your eyes and look closer
i'm not between you and your ambition
i am a poster girl with no poster
i am thirty-two flavors and then some
and i'm beyond your peripheral vision
so you might wanna turn your head
cuz someday you might find you are hungry
eating most of the words you just said

both my parents taught me about good will
and i have done well by their names
just the kindness i've lavished on strangers
is more than i can explain
still there's many who've turned out their porch lights
just so i would think they were not home
and hid in the dark of their windows
til i passed and left them alone

god help you if you are an ugly girl
course too pretty is also your doom
cuz everyone harbors a secret hatred
for the prettiest girl in the room
and god help you if you are a phoenix
and you dare to rise up from the ash
a thousand eyes will smolder with jealousy
while you are just flying past

i never tried to give my life meaning
by demeaning you
and i would like to state for the record
i did everything that i could do
i'm not saying that i'm a saint
i just don't wanna live that way

no, i will never be a saint
but i will always say

squint your eyes and look closer
i'm not between you and your ambition
i am a poster girl with no poster
i am thirty-two flavors and then some
and i'm beyond your peripheral vision
so you might wanna turn your head
cuz someday you might find you are starving
and eating all of the words that you said

hearse

i don't wanna strive for nothin, anymore
i just wanna lie here with you
keep the wolves outside the door
there is nothin in this world you could ever show me
that could ever matter more

little baby, in the next room dreamin
is just icing on the cake
there is nothing like dancin
our dance of give and take
one step forward
one step sideways
that helpless feeling
when the earth shakes

i will always be your lover
even after our atoms are dispersed
we'll be pushing up daisies
and my crush will just be gettin worse
and i will follow you into the next life
like a dog chasing after a hearse

i just don't wanna strive for nothin, anymore
i just wanna lie here with you
keep the wolves outside the door
there is nothin in this world you could ever show me
that could ever matter more

angry anymore

growing up it was just me and my mom against the world
and all my sympathies were with her, when i was a little girl
but now i've seen both my parents play out the hands that they were dealt
and as each year goes by, i know more about how my father must have felt

i just want you to understand
that i know what all the fighting was for
and i just want you to understand
that i'm not angry anymore
no, i'm not angry anymore

she taught me how to wage a cold war with quiet charm
but i just want to walk through my life unarmed
to accept and just get by, like my father learned to do
but without all the acceptance and getting by that got my father through

i just want you to understand
that i know what all the fighting was for
and i just want you to understand
that i'm not angry anymore
no, i'm not angry anymore

night falls, like people into love
and we generate our own light to compensate for the lack of light from above
and every time we fight, a cold wind blows our way
but we can learn, like the trees, how to bend
how to sway and say

i, i think i understand

what all this fighting is for
and baby, i just want you to understand
that i'm not angry anymore
no, i'm not angry anymore

out of habit

the butter melts out of habit
the toast isn't even warm
the waitress and the man in the plaid shirt
play out a scene they've played
so many times before
i am watching the sun
stumble home in the morning
from a bar on the east side of town
and the coffee is just water dressed in brown

beautiful but boring
he visited me yesterday
and he noticed my fingers
and he asked me if i would play
and i didn't really care a lot
but i couldn't think of a reason why not
i said, if you don't come any closer
i don't mind if you stay
you know, my thighs have been involved
in many accidents
and now i can't get insured
and i don't need to be lured by you
my cunt is built
like a wound that won't heal
and now you don't have to ask
cuz you know how i feel

art is why i get up in the morning
but my definition ends there
it doesn't seem fair
that i'm living for something
i can't even define
and there you are, right there

in the meantime
you know, i don't want to play for you anymore
you show me what you can do
you tell me, what are you here for?
i want my old friends
i want my old face
i want my old mind
fuck this time and place

the butter melts out of habit
the toast isn't even warm

every state line

i got pulled over in west texas
so they could look inside my car
he said, are you an american citizen?
i said, yes sir, so far
they made sure i wasn't smuggling
someone in from mexico
someone willing to settle for america
because there's nowhere else to go

every state line
there's a new set of laws
and every policeman
comes equipped with extended claws
there's a thousand shades of white
and a thousand shades of black
but the same rule always applies:
smile pretty and watch your back

i broke down in louisiana
and i had to thumb a ride
got in the first car that pulled over
you can't be picky in the middle of the night
he said, baby do you like to fool around?
baby do you like to be touched?
i said, maybe some other time
fuck you very much

every state line
there's a new set of laws
and every policeman
comes equipped with extended claws
there's a thousand shades of white
and a thousand shades of black
but the same rule always applies:
smile pretty and watch your back

in the middle of alabama
they stare at me wherever i go
i don't think they like my haircut
i don't think they like my clothes
i can't wait to get back to new york city
where at least when i walk down the street
no one ever hesitates
to tell me exactly what they think of me

and every state line
there's a new set of laws
every policeman
comes equipped with extended claws
there's a thousand shades of white
and a thousand shades of black
but the same rule always applies:
smile pretty and watch your back

a little town in pennsylvania
there was snow on the ground
i parked it in an empty lot
where there was no one else around
but i guess i was taking up too much space
as i was trying to get some sleep
cuz an officer came by anyway
and told me i had to leave

and every state line
there's a new set of laws
and every policeman
comes equipped with extended claws
there's a thousand shades of white
and a thousand shades of black
but the same rule always applies:
smile pretty and watch your back

hide 'n' seek

me and all the kids from the neighborhood
we play out in the street all summer long
the rule was, we had to go home at night
when the streetlights came on
we were oblivious to the rest of the world
we'd hold up the cars in the street
we'd always play boys against girls
and both sides would cheat

strange men would stop their cars at the curb
and say hey sweetheart, come here
and i'd go up to the window
and they'd have their dick in their hand and a sick little sneer
i'd say here we go again
yeah, ok this time, you win
and i would feel dirty and i'd feel ashamed
but i wouldn't let it stop my game

we would play hide and go seek
the territory would be the whole block
sometimes the older boys, when they'd find you
they wouldn't wanna tag you
they'd just wanna talk
they'd say, what would you do for a quarter?
come on, we don't have that much time
and i'd think a minute and i'd say
ok, give me the quarter first
fine
this time you win
here we go again
and i would feel dirty and i would feel ashamed
but i wouldn't let it stop my game

i remember my first trip alone on the greyhound bus
a man put his hands on me as soon as night fell
i remember when i was leaving, how excited i was
i remember when i arrived, i didn't feel so well
i remember the teacher at school
who got me so sick and scared
that i went into the bathroom
and threw up in my hair
and i could go on but it gets worse
and i should probably stop there

girl, the next time he wants to know
what your problem is
girl, next time he wants to know
where the anger comes from
just tell him that this time the problem's his
just tell him, the anger just comes
it just comes

out of range (acoustic)

just the thought of our bed
makes me crumble like the plaster
where you punched the wall beside my head
and i try to draw the line
but it ends up running down the middle of me
most of the time

boys get locked up in some prison
girls get locked up in some house
and it don't matter if it's a warden
or a lover or a spouse
you just can't talk to um
you just can't reason
you just can't leave
and you just can't please um

i was locked
into being my mother's daughter
i was just eating bread and water
thinking nothing ever changes
then i was shocked
to see the mistakes of each generation
will just fade like a radio station
if you drive out of range

if you're not angry
then you're just stupid or you don't care
how else can you react
when you know something's so unfair?
when the men of the hour
can kill half the world in war
or make them slaves to a superpower
and then let them die poor

i was locked
into being my mother's daughter
i was just eating bread and water
thinking nothing ever changes
then i was shocked
to see the mistakes of each generation
will just fade like a radio station
if you drive out of range

just the thought of our bed
makes me crumble like the plaster
where you punched the wall beside my head
and i try to draw the line
but it ends up running down the middle of me
most of the time

baby, i love you
that's why i'm leaving
there's just no talking to you
and there's just no pleasing you
and i care enough
that i'm mad
that half the world don't even know
what they could'a had

i was locked
into being my mother's daughter
i was just eating bread and water
thinking nothing ever changes
then i was shocked
to see the mistakes of each generation
will just fade like a radio station
if you drive
you just gotta drive
out of range

shameless

i cannot name this
i cannot explain this
and i really don't want to
just call me shameless
can't even slow this down
let alone stop this
and i keep looking around
but i cannot top this

if i had any sense
i guess i'd fear this
i guess i'd keep it down
so no one would hear this
i guess i'd shut my mouth
and rethink a minute
but i can't shut it now
cuz there's something in it

we're in a room without a door
and i am sure without a doubt
they're gonna want to know how we got in here
and they're gonna want to know
how we plan to get out
we'd better have a good explanation
for all the fun that we had
cuz they are coming for us, baby
and they are going to be mad

yeah, they're going to be mad at us

this is my skeleton
this is the skin it's in
that is, according to light

and gravity
i'll take off my disguise
the mask you met me in
cuz i got something
for you to see
just gimme your skeleton
give me the skin it's in
yeah, baby, this is you
according to me
and i never avert my eyes
i never compromise
so never, never mind
the poetry

i gotta cover my butt cuz i covet
another man's wife
i gotta divide my emotions
into wrong and right
and then i get to see how close i can get to it
without giving in
and i get to rub up against it
till i break the skin
rub up against it
till i break the skin

they're gonna be mad at us
they're gonna be mad at me and you
they're gonna be mad at us
and all the things we like to do

just please don't name this
please don't explain this
just blame it all on me
say i was shameless
say i couldn't slow it down
let alone stop it

and say you just hung around
cuz you couldn't top it

adam and eve

tonight you stooped to my level
i am your mangy little whore
now you're trying to find your underwear
and then your socks and then the door
and you're trying to find a reason
why you have to leave
but i know it's cuz you think you're adam
and you think i'm eve

you rhapsodize about beauty
and my eyes glaze
everything i love is ugly
i mean really, you'd be amazed
just do me a favor
it's the least that you can do
just don't treat me like i am
something that happened to you

i am truly sorry about all this

but you put a tiny pin prick
in my big red balloon
and as i slowly start to exhale
that's when you leave the room
i did not design this game
i did not name the stakes
i just happen to like apples
and i am not afraid of snakes

i am truly sorry about all this
i envy you your ignorance
i hear that it's bliss

so i let go the ratio
of things said to things heard
as i leave you to your garden
and the beauty you preferred
and i wonder what of this will have meaning
for you, when you've left it all behind
i guess i'll even wonder
if you meant it
at the time

the million you never made

the air comes off the ocean
and the city smells fishy
the air is full of fish and mystery
whispering who? what? when?
and i'm warning you i'm weightless
and the wind is always shifting
so don't hang anything on me
if you ever want to see it again
i'm telling you i'm different
than you think i am

you can dangle your carrot
but i ain't gonna reach for it
cuz i need both my hands
to play my guitar
life is a sleazy stranger
who looks vaguely familiar
flirting with a bimbo named disaster
at the end of the bar
i'm telling you i'm different
than you are

at night when you're asleep
self hatred's gonna creep in
you can blame it on the devil
the one whose bed you sleep in
don't tell me what they did to you
as though you had no choice
isn't that your picture?
isn't that your voice?
if you don't live what you sing about
your mirror is going to find out

i'd like to go to all the pretty parties
where all the pretty people go
and i ain't really all that pretty
but nobody will know
cuz everybody loves you
when you're a star
and nobody questions
what it takes to go that far
life is a sleazy stranger
and this is his favorite bar

and no, i don't prefer obscurity
but i'm an idealistic girl
and i wouldn't work for you
no matter what you paid
i may not be able
to change the whole fucking world
but i can be the million
that you never made
yeah i can be the million
you never made
you are looking at the million
that you never made

the atom

the glory of the atom
begs a reverent word
the primary design
of the whole universe
yes, let us sing its praises
let us bow our heads in prayer
at the magnificent consciousness
incarnate there

the smallest unit of matter
with its orbiting electrons
echoing off the solar system
like a hawk in the hills at dawn
the smallest unit of matter
uniting bird and rock and tree
and you and me

oh holy is the atom
the truly intelligent design
to which all of evolution
is graciously aligned
the one single structure
to which everything distills
the air
the wood smoke there
and the hills

leave me here surrounded
by everything that's real
far outside the boundaries
of the digitized ordeal
leave me here awake
leave me here to heal

human beings are a cross
between monkeys and ants
you can see us from your spaceship
melting the ice caps
with our arrogance
summon a congress of angels
dressed in riot gear
we got ourselves a serious situation
down here

i have this great great uncle
who worked on the atomic bomb
he got a nobel prize in physics
and a place in this song
and i bet there were no windows
and no women in the room
when they applied themselves
to the pure science of boom

yes, messing with the atom
is the highest form of blasphemy
whether you are making weapons
or simple electricity
someone fashion me a pulpit
i have been called to engage
with the maniacal heretics
of the nuclear age

let the religious get religion
let consumers get a clue
let scientists get perspective
let activists get their due
let industry get a conscience
let the earth inherit the meek
let the divinity of nature speak

the glory of the atom
begs a reverent word
the primary design
of the whole universe
yes, let us sing its praises
let us bow our heads in prayer
at the magnificent consciousness
incarnate there

binary

where are my sisters
where are my brothers
where is my family
who takes care of each other

in the blue glow of gizmos
lurk despots in diapers
and cyborgs with bullhorns
and crackpots and snipers
like robots, so cold
with such ease, they dismiss you
sooner fuck you than kiss you
sooner kick you and diss you
they got networks, like insects
with webs of deception
they'll trap you, cocoon you
like a department of corrections
they come in all colors
and sexes and creeds
they got all kinda issues
they got all kinda needs
little laboratory monkeys
raised with no hugging
just a wire cage mamma
and lab coats mugging
i feel your anger
i feel your pain
i feel the aching hole in your soul
that can't be named
consciousness is binary
consciousness is spinning
consciousness is a circuit
when consciousness is winning
consciousness is binary

consciousness is spinning
consciousness is a circuit
when consciousness is winning

you gotta complete the circuit
alone, there's just no knowing
yeah, energy is destructive
unless it is flowing
in the connection lies the spark
in the connection lies the art
you gotta be up in someone's countenance
conversing with their heart
you gotta complete the circuit
not just with human beings
with the sky above you
with the earth beneath your feet
when you complete the circuit
with everything that lives
borders get blurry
and the rest is adjectives
borders get blurry
and the rest is adjectives
consciousness is binary
consciousness is spinning
consciousness is a circuit
when consciousness is winning
where are my sisters
where are my brothers
where is my family
who takes care of each other?

little plastic castle

in a coffee shop
in a city
which is every coffee shop
in every city
on a day
which is every day
i picked up a magazine
which is every magazine
read a story
and then forgot it
right away

and they say goldfish
have no memory
i guess their lives
are much like mine
and the little plastic castle
is a surprise
every time
and it's hard to say
if they're happy
but they don't seem
much to mind

from the shape
of your shaved head
i recognized
your silhouette
as you walked out
of the sun
and sat down
and the sight of your
sleepy smile

eclipsed all the other people
as they paused
to sneer at the two girls
from out of town

i said, look at you
this morning
you are, by far
the cutest
but be careful
getting coffee
i think these people
wanna shoot us
or maybe there's some kinda
local competition here
to see who can
be the rudest

people talk
about my image
like i come
in two dimensions
like lipstick
is a sign
of my declining mind
like what i happen
to be wearing
the day that someone
takes a picture
is my new statement
for all of womankind

i wish they could
see us now
in leather bras
and rubber shorts

like some ridiculous
new team uniform
for some ridiculous
new sport
quick someone
call the girl police
and file a report

in a coffee shop
in a city
which is every coffee shop
in every city
on a day
which is everyday

willing to fight

the windows of my soul
are made of one way glass
don't bother looking into my eyes
if there's something you want to know
just ask
i got a deadbolt stroll
where i'm going is clear
i won't wait for you to wonder
i'll just tell you why i'm here

cuz i know the biggest crime
is to just throw up your hands
say, this has nothing to do with me
i just want to live as comfortably as i can
you got to look outside your eyes
you got to think outside your brain
you got to walk outside your life
to where the neighborhood changes

tell me, who's your boogie man?
that's who i will be
you don't have to like me for who i am
but we'll see what you're made of
by what you make of me
you know, i think it's absurd
that you think i am the derelict daughter
you know, i fight fire with words
words are hotter than flames
words are wetter than water

i got friends all over this country
i got friends in other countries too
i got friends i haven't met yet

i got friends i never knew
i got lovers who's eyes
i've only seen at a glance
i got strangers for great grandchildren
i got strangers for ancestors
i was a long time coming
i'll be a long time gone
you got your whole life to do something
(and that's not very long)
why don't you give me a call
when you decide you're willing to fight
for what you think is real
for what you think is right

if he tries anything

i'm invincible
so are you
we do all the things
they say we can't do
we walk around
in the middle of the night
and if it's too far to walk
we just hitch a ride

we got rings of dirt
around our necks
we talk like auctioneers
and we bounce like checks
we smell like shit
still when we walk down the street
all the boys line up
to throw themselves at our feet

i say, i think he likes you
you say, i think he do too
i say, go and get him, girl
before he gets you
i'll be watching you
from the wings
i will come to your rescue
if he tries anything

it's a long long road
it's a big big world
we are wise wise women
we are giggling girls
we both carry a smile
to show when we're pleased

we both carry a switchblade
in our sleeves

i'll tell you one thing
i'm going to make noise when i go down
for ten square blocks
they're gonna know i died
all the goddesses will come up
to the ripped screen door
and say, what do you want dear?
and i'll say, i want inside

i say, i think he likes you
you say, i think he do too
i say, go and get him, girl
before he gets you
i'll be watching you
from the wings
i will come to your rescue
if he tries anything

hour follows hour

hour follows hour
like water follows water
everything is governed
by the rule of one thing leads to another
and you can't really place blame
cuz blame is much too messy
some was bound to get on you
while you were trying to put it on me

don't fool yourself
into thinking things are simple
nobody's lying
and still the stories don't line up
why do you try to hold on to
what you'll never get a hold on?
you wouldn't try to put the ocean
in a paper cup

i have had something to prove
as long as i've had something that needs improvement
and you know, that every time i move
i make a woman's movement
first you decide what you've gotta do
then you go out and do it
and maybe the most that we can do
is just to see each other thru it

hour follows hour
like water in a river
and from one to the next
we don't know what each hour will deliver
we just call it like we see it
we call it out loud as we can

and then afterwards we call it all water
over the dam

and maybe the moral high ground
ain't as high as it seems
maybe we are both good people
who've done some bad things
i just hope it was ok
i know it wasn't perfect
i hope in the end we can laugh and say
it was all worth it

i have had something to prove
as long as i've had something that needs improvement
and you know, every time i move
i make a woman's movement
first you decide what you've gotta do
then you go out and do it
and maybe the most that we can do
is just to see each other thru it

we make our own gravity
to give weight to things
and then things fall and they break
and gravity sings
we can only hold so much is what i figure
we try and keep our eye on the big picture
and the picture keeps getting bigger

and too much is how i love you
but too well is how i know you
and i've got nothing to prove this time
just something to show you
i guess i just wanted you to see
that it was all worth it to me

reckoning

you can doubt anything
if you think about it long enough
cuz what happened always adjusts
to fit what happened after that
and it's hard to feel like you are free
when all you seem to do is referee
remember when it was just you and me
steppin up to bat?

and win or lose, just that you choose
this little war
is what kills you
and either/or it's that this war
is maybe also what thrills you

we thought we left possession behind
but truth is, i was yours and you were mine
and now i've replayed a thousand times
exactly what was said
cuz nothing is as it appears
in the funhouse mirrors of your fears
on the roller coaster of all these years
with your hands above your head

and win or lose, just that you choose
this little war
is what kills you
and either/or it's that this war
is maybe also what thrills you

i don't care how fast you run
just tell me, baby, that when you're done
with your little marathon

you still got cab fare home
cuz the finish line is a shifty thing
and what is life but reckoning?
and, you know
you are still the song i sing
to myself
when i'm alone

and win or lose, just that we choose
this little war is what kills us
and either/or it's that this war
is maybe also what thrills us

the knowing

i have a name
and my name has a story
i have a look
a sound
a smell
a shape
a size
i have a color to my hair
my skin
my eyes

but this is not all of who i am
underneath this is something more
all of these things are just what's showing
underneath all that i know is the knowing
underneath all that i know is the knowing

i have a favorite blanket
it's a little torn
i have a family
and a place where i was born
i have a favorite song
and a favorite food
i have a favorite game
depending on my mood

but this is not all of who i am
underneath this is something more
all of these things are just what's showing
underneath all that i know is the knowing
underneath all that i know is the knowing

i have a life that i'm here to live
i have gifts that i'm here to give
i have friends and with my friends, i have fun
i have a love of the wind and of the sun

yes, i can take heart in what's showing
knowing it's all a part of the knowing
yes, i can take part in what's showing
knowing we're all a part of the knowing

i have beliefs and someday
those beliefs might change
i have blocks that i like to arrange
and rearrange
there are things that i'm told
and things that i learn
there are skills i've practiced
and praise i've earned

but this is not all of who i am
underneath this is something more
all of these things are just what's showing
underneath all that i know is the knowing
underneath all that i know is the knowing
underneath all that i know is the knowing